MW00561798

◆ © BUD LEE

Northern Kentucky

LOOKING *to the* NEW MILLENNIUM

Northern Kentucky

LOOKING *to the* NEW MILLENNIUM

ART DIRECTION BY ENRIQUE ESPINOSA

Introduction by

Steve Cauthen

Sponsored by the
Northern Kentucky
Chamber of Commerce

Table of Contents

LIBRARY OF CONGRESS CATALOGING-IN-PUBLICATION DATA IS AVAILABLE ON PAGE 203.

COURTESY STEVE CAUTHEN

© ALLSPORT

BY THE TIME I WAS READY TO END MY MY racing career in 1992, I had already made the decision to return to the beautiful bluegrass of Northern Kentucky, where I was born and grew up. Now, just a few miles from there, I raise horses on a farm that's my ideal. And it's here that I plan to stay.

When I first started riding, though, I had different plans. I left my little home town of Verona thinking that I'd live somewhere else for the rest of my life. I thought Verona was a great place to grow up, but I had big ideas about all these foreign countries—I thought that there had to be some superb place somewhere, and soon I'd find it.

And in truth, I *could* have made my home anywhere in the world. Fame found me early in life, and my riding career took me around the globe and introduced me to people from all walks of life, from royalty to simple farmers. But it was here in Northern Kentucky near Covington that I would again make my home, to raise my own family and build upon the roots that I had never strayed too far away from.

The perspective of my earlier career has helped me to appreciate my home in a way that others can't. Northern Kentucky holds all for me that life needs to hold. Winston Churchill is widely quoted as having said that the important thing is not to make a living, but to make a life. ☛

▼ © TOM UHLMAN

I made a living on horseback at tracks and venues around the world; I am making a life here amid the bluegrass of my youth.

A bit of background might help me make my point: People make a big deal about how I won the Triple Crown when I was only 18—the youngest rider ever to achieve that honor. That year, 1978, I rode Affirmed to victory in the Kentucky Derby, the Belmont Stakes, and the Preakness. Although many people treated me like I had just burst onto the racing scene, like most "overnight sensations" there was a great deal of preparation that went on before this. I was doing very well before I won the Triple Crown. I started as a professional jockey when I was 16, and had been working toward this ultimate prize since I was 12. The first six months that I was a professional, I won a couple of hundred races. The next year, I won 480 races and was the leading rider in the country. So, I wasn't a complete unknown when I won the Triple Crown the following year. By the time I went to Europe a year later, I was well known throughout the racing community.

First, I raced in England. Not only was this country appealing for all the reasons that draw millions of tourists each year, but it's simply a wonderful place to race. There's a lot of pag-

© DOROTHY B. JOHNSTON

eantry surrounding horse racing. Many of the people involved are royalty. At a race, you'll see the queen, rock stars, right on down the line to just plain farmers who are really into it. Racing is a major sport there. Second only to "football"—soccer—it's part of the national fiber.

I soon began racing in France, Germany, Italy, Ireland, Sweden, Norway, Hong Kong, Japan, Australia, Argentina, South Africa, Puerto Rico—around the world. Wherever I went, I kept looking and thinking that this city—or that country—would be a nice place to make a home after I finished my career as a jockey. As I weighed the different advantages and assets, I realized that Northern Kentucky is pretty hard to beat when you talk about the whole picture. So, in the end, I came back here to an area that includes Boone, Campbell, and Kenton counties—names so familiar to me.

While my family connections and personal history played a big role in my decision to return and settle down here, there's another overwhelming factor why I live here: Being in the horse business makes this a natural location for me. Northern Kentucky is the center of the horse breeding industry for the entire world. ☛

RABBIT HASH IRON WORK
STOVES • GIFTS • CRAFTS •

© DALE VOELKER

I'm far from the first person to experience the lure of this part of the country. Northern Kentucky enjoys a rich and, for outsiders, surprisingly colorful history. The popular myth among Cincinnati residents—who have long referred to Northern Kentucky dwellers as "briar-hoppers"—seems to be that those who live in Boone, Campbell, or Kenton counties are there because they somehow don't fit with the sophisticated way of life in the big city. If you take a quick look at the origins of Northern Kentucky, though, you find out that this is not even close to the truth.

It turns out that Cincinnati and parts of Northern Kentucky—notably Covington—were settled at about the same time. Some historians believe that rather than Cincinnati, Northern Kentucky was, ironically, the destination for the waves of Scotch-Irish "Yankees" and later of German and Irish settlers who came here in the early and middle 19th century. Some traveled down the Ohio River, likening it to the Rhine back in the old country, while others made the long journey upriver from New Orleans to what they realized was outstanding agricultural and pasture land.

Most of Kentucky had few such immigrants. Yet Covington, Newport, and Louisville had immigrant populations that stood at 20 percent in 1900. German was still spoken in many churches in the area until about the time of World War I, and both Irish and German newspapers were published here until the 1930s.

The presence of these immigrants is still felt strongly. Architecture throughout Northern Kentucky's cities is influenced by different European cultures. In Covington, MainStrasse Village and Goebel Park, with its distinctively Bavarian Gothic Carroll Chimes Bell Tower, are examples of the strong influence of German immigrants. Covington is also home to the Cathedral Basilica of the Assumption, a Gothic treasure that is fashioned after Notre Dame de Paris.

Throughout the 19th century, Cincinnati grew factories and banks and houses; Northern Kentucky grew casinos and farms and horses. By the middle of the 1800s, a pattern had ☛

▲ © MARK BOWEN / 2 GUYS AND SOME SLIDES

emerged whereby citizens of Cincinnati came across the river to gamble at one of the casinos or betting parlors of Newport or Covington. Meanwhile, Northern Kentuckians went to Cincinnati to work, to buy things, and to enjoy the cultural events that were becoming established in the city. These weren't all laborers or factory workers; a good many prosperous burghers who worked in Cincinnati built fine homes along Mansion Hill, directly across the Ohio River in Covington. Workers tended to live in the more modest row houses that still stand several blocks away from the river.

So heavy was the traffic that a bridge was built in 1868, much earlier than most people would guess, between Cincinnati and Covington. Today, this bridge—the John A. Roebling Suspension Bridge—is noteworthy for being a kind of prototype for the Brooklyn Bridge. It's still heavily traveled, and deposits Northern Kentuckians right at the doors of old Riverfront Stadium, now known as Cinergy Field, home of the Cincinnati Reds and Bengals. Today, though, there are four other bridges linking Cincinnati with Covington and Newport, making quick river crossings a breeze.

The gambling and bawdy reputation of Northern Kentucky endured for decades, but came to an end more than half a century ago. No longer was the area seen as a place for Cincinnatians to go and have a wild time. During World War II and in the years shortly after, it came to be seen as a perfect place for all kinds of growth. The army air corps came looking for a bomber base, and ended up building a field that would evolve into today's massive Cincinnati/Northern Kentucky International Airport. Roads were built, evolving into today's elaborate network of interstate highways that link the region with convenient spokes and arteries. Towns and villages grew into cities, and buildings began to reach skyward. ☛

Lake Central
AIRLINES

AMERICAN AIRLINES

▲ © PAULA NORTON / NORTON PHOTOSTOCK

And families began to move to Northern Kentucky—just as original settlers had—to work and live. No longer would briarhopper jokes hold sway. Northern Kentucky, over the past 50 years, has continued to grow into its own, becoming a prosperous and self-sustained region. True, we still rely on Cincinnati for a good many things. But the difference is that Cincinnati now also relies, heavily, on us.

Northern Kentucky is obviously a very popular part of the world right now and it is developing so rapidly that it's easy to lose sight of the many assets that have supported its rise to prominence.

For one thing, the region's central location is obviously a big factor in its ever increasing development. A lot of businesses have sprouted up here largely because of the easy access they have to so many other parts of the country. Major companies that have come to the area in recent years include the Internal Revenue Service, Delta Air Lines, Fidelity Investments, The Gap/Banana Republic, Comair, Mazak Corporation, Newport Steel, Duro Bag Manufacturing, DHL Airways, and scores of others too numerous to mention.

A lot of the new businesses have moved here because of the quality of living. Others have come because of the close proximity to Cincinnati. And, undeniably, even more have come to take ☛

▲ © WILLIAM V. WEST

advantage of the relatively new Cincinnati/Northern Kentucky airport, a Delta hub and one of the busiest airports in the country. The facility also serves as the major sorting hub for DHL Airways, one of the country's largest courier and package delivery services.

Along with the businesses have come scores of people moving to the area to work. More jobs, more housing, more roads, more of everything. Those who come here are so refreshed by the people they run into and meet that the rough edges they might have started to get from city life seem to kind of smooth out a little bit.

There's still a real sense that Northern Kentucky is not a part of "urban everywhere." When I was growing up, it was pretty much a rural area, at least compared to what it is now. My farm is just far enough away that it still feels like we're out in the bluegrass country. But the city environment just seems to keep moving our way very quickly and, with that, come some things that you love and some things that you like to be closer to—like a grocery store! At any rate, the result is that we've really got the best of several worlds—a country lifestyle, with all the amenities of small-town living.

But it's a little bit confusing telling people from outside the area just what comprises Northern Kentucky. You hear it referred to in recent slogans as "the southern side of Cincinnati," which is an accurate geographic description, but doesn't go quite far enough. Within its three counties are the individual towns and cities that are the backbone of our communities— ☛

SUPERLINER
Amtrak

IBRARY

▲ © MARK BOWEN / 2 GUYS AND SOME SLIDES
◀ © PAUL A NORTON / NORTON PHOTOSTOCK

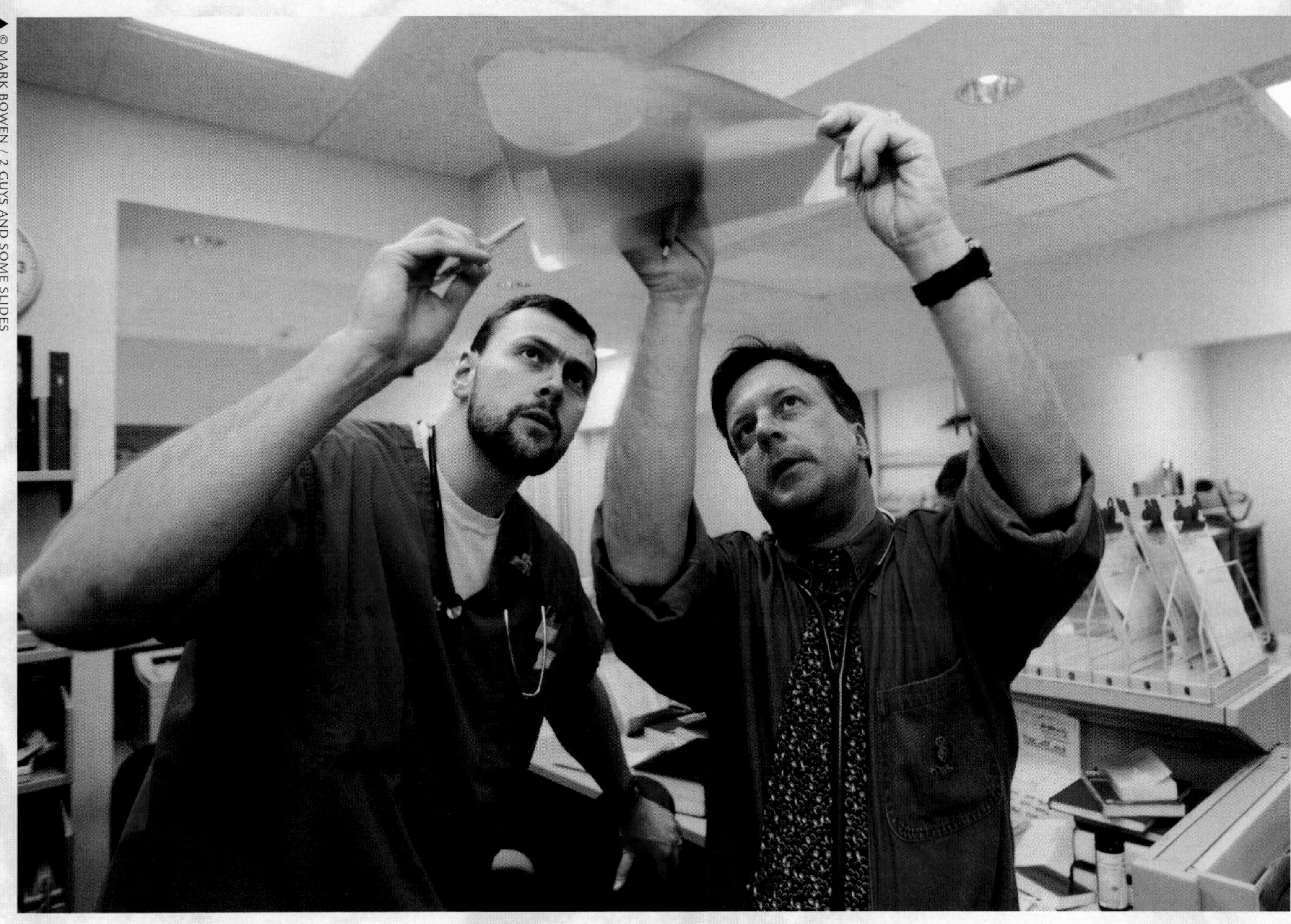

Covington, Florence, Bellevue, Erlanger, Fort Mitchell, Burlington, Fort Thomas, Independence, Newport, and historic Rabbit Hash (no fooling).

The nearly 600 square miles that make up the region are home to a population of more than 300,000 people served by more than 30 hospitals, 80 public schools, 40 libraries, and lots of new, affordable housing. Today, signs throughout the region will direct you to one new subdivision after another.

Our universities and colleges are some of the best the nation has to offer. Northern Kentucky University opened in Highland Heights in 1970 and proved to be a catalyst for a lot of the community-building activities that have occurred recently. In addition to Thomas More College in Covington, which grew from a school founded in 1921, NKU serves as one more reason why people no longer need to go downstate or across the river to get a quality education. NKU's cultural and leisure-time activities have also done a lot to foster a sense that Northern Kentucky is a unique place.

Furthering that spirit of community are the many attractions in the city of Covington. The Behringer-Crawford Museum is a natural and cultural history museum devoted to preserving the area's past. The Carnegie Arts Center, built nearly 100 years ago, is both an art gallery ☛

© MARK BOWEN / 2 GUYS AND SOME SLIDES

and a theater. Covington Landing has all sorts of shops and restaurants, all of them floating on a huge, bargelike vessel on the Ohio River. And, BB Riverboats offers daily cruises on the river.

Although Northern Kentucky takes pride in maintaining a separate identity, nowhere is the bond with neighboring Cincinnati more apparent than in the many leisure, recreational, and sporting attractions the big city has to offer. Paramount's Kings Island amusement park, one of the best in this part of the country, is always fun. The Cincinnati Zoo and Botanical Garden, with its white Bengal tigers, is a special treat. The Cincinnati Art Museum, the Cinergy Children's Museum, and a whole calendar of concerts, symphony orchestra performances, and ballets give us plenty to do.

Sports are a big deal in this part of the country. We're just minutes away from the Reds and the Bengals in Cincinnati, who play across the bridge in Cinergy Field. The University of Kentucky (just down the road in Lexington), the University of Louisville, and the University of Cincinnati are all major forces in college basketball.

And (close to my heart), Northern Kentucky is in the midst of the country's most active horse racing venues. Within easy reach are many of the top-rated tracks and facilities—I serve as

▲ © MARK BOWEN / 2 GUYS AND SOME SLIDES

vice president of Turfway Park in Florence; Churchill Downs is only 60 miles away in Louisville; and many farms and facilities dot the bluegrass country that spreads out around Lexington.

There's nothing more beautiful than Lexington. The Kentucky Horse Park there is an educational theme park that includes the International Museum of the Horse, live horse shows, and some 40 different breeds for viewing and petting. But even if you don't like horses, there's nothing more beautiful than to drive by the farms, with their fences and the barns that look like houses. All of these are idyllic places for anyone who loves the way of life that is associated with horses and racing.

From a tradition that dates back 200 years, Northern Kentucky has maintained this connection with horses and the land in a way that makes the area especially attractive to me. The slowly rising and falling hills, the bluegrass, the favorable climate, the rich soil with lots of calcium and phosphorus—all are ideal conditions for raising and breeding horses.

Which is to say, ideal for me.

▲ © ROGER BICKEL

▲ © DAN TYE

WITH ITS SISTER COMMUNITY of Cincinnati (OPPOSITE) along the banks of the Ohio River to the north, the city of Covington (ABOVE) is the gateway to the rapidly growing region known as Northern Kentucky.

© BUD LEE

THE CHRISTMAS SHOPPE
Main Street 431-0032
HAUS
BEER · WINE · SPIRITS
TWO
HOUR
PARKING

© ANNE PINNAU

▶ © ANNE PINNAU

ACTIVITY ALONG MAINSTRASSE Village—a five-block area of restored, 19th-century, German structures in Covington—includes sidewalk shopping and the Second Sunday Antiques show, a monthly (except September) event near Goebel Park.

FULL QUART
CONTENTS 32 FL. OZ.
CINCINNATI'S
PRIDE
BRAND
BEER
BREWED AND BOTTLED BY
BAVARIAN BREWING CO.
INCORPORATED
COVINGTON, KY.
INTERNAL REVENUE TAX PAID
DOES NOT CONTAIN MORE THAN 3.2% OF ALCOHOL BY WT.

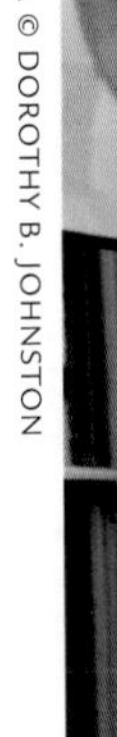

▲ © CINCINNATI MUSEUM CENTER

Nothing washes down a steaming bowl of three-way chili better than a cold brew in the company of friends.

LARRY'S
ALL AMERICAN
CAFE

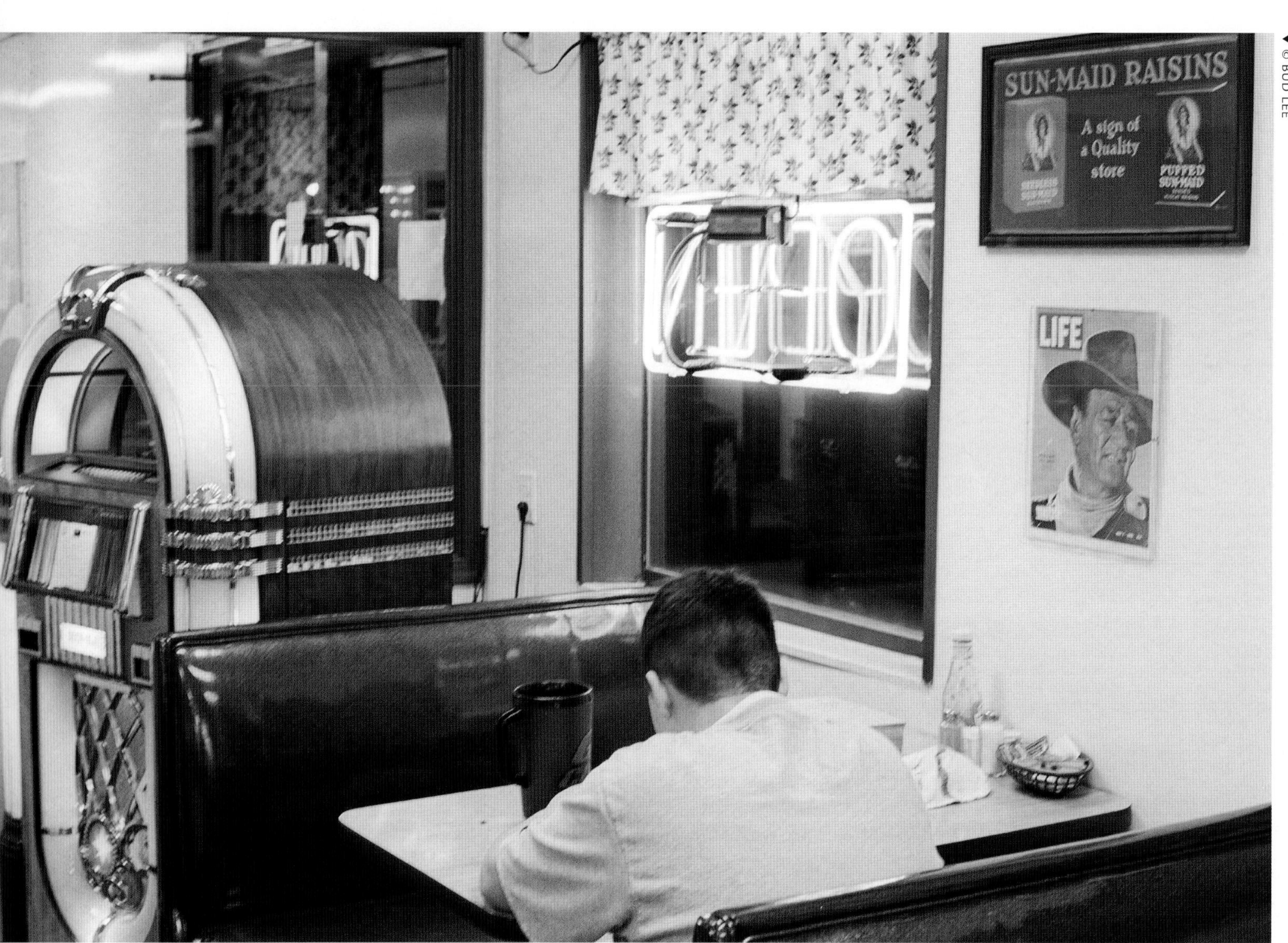
SUN-MAID RAISINS
A sign of
a Quality
store
PUFFED
SUN-MAID
LIFE

▼ © BUD LEE

▲ © BUD LEE

THERE'S AN OLD-FASHIONED quality to life in Northern Kentucky, where carefully selected tunes from the jukebox can lead to hours whiled away in the local diner.

▼ © BUD LEE

▼ © JIM HURTLE

▲ © BUD LEE

NOT MUCH SAYS "AMERICANA" like a picturesque storefront. The antiquated Rabbit Hash General Store (OPPOSITE), listed on the National Register of Historic Places, has been in operation since 1831.

▲ © BUD LEE

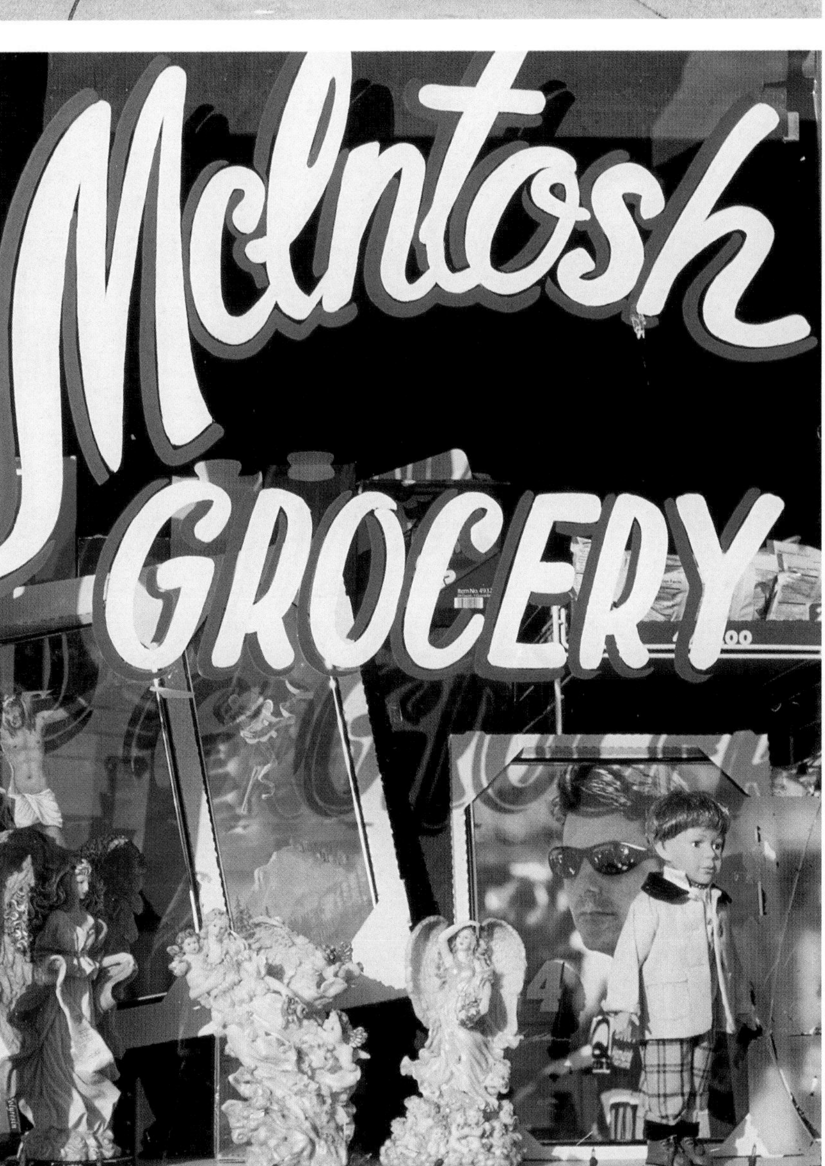

© BUD LEE

© BUD LEE

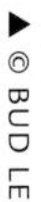

▲ © BUD LEE

▲ © BUD LEE

THE BUCOLIC SETTINGS OF NORTHern Kentucky lend themselves well to relaxing times with friends and family.

▲ © CHRIS CONE

▲ © DALE VOELKER

WITH ITS SIGHTS TRAINED ON Cincinnati's skyline, an old cannon assumes its position in a Civil War encampment re-creation depicting life at the Newport Barracks. Local battlefield reenactments extend to the Revolutionary War as well (BOTTOM).

▲ © DOROTHY B. JOHNSTON

PATRIOTISM KNOWS NO AGE boundaries as Northern Kentuckians turn out for Fourth of July celebrations.

© DAN TYE

© RICK NORTON / NORTON PHOTOSTOCK

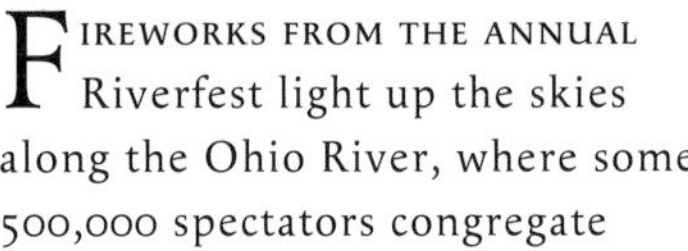

FIREWORKS FROM THE ANNUAL Riverfest light up the skies along the Ohio River, where some 500,000 spectators congregate each year for the festivities (OPPOSITE AND ABOVE RIGHT). Covington, Newport, and Cincinnati all take part in the event, which celebrated its 27th birthday in 1999. With its Ferris wheel and other rides, a local Oktoberfest also draws quite a crowd (ABOVE LEFT).

▲ © DAN TYE

PLANNING FOR AN EXPLOSIVE celebration? Local fireworks stores will ensure you have an ample supply of the latest in pyrotechnics (PAGES 56 AND 57).

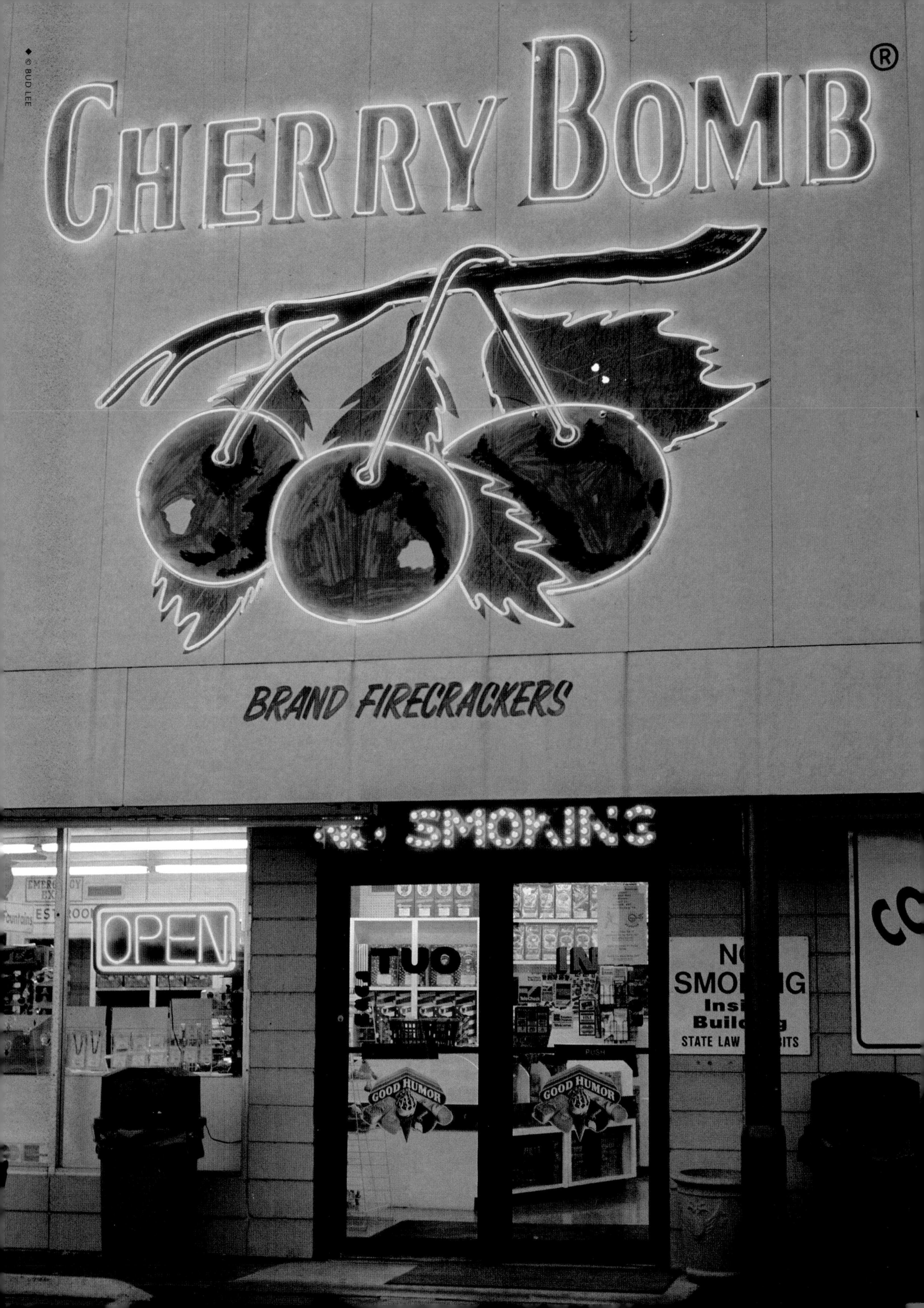

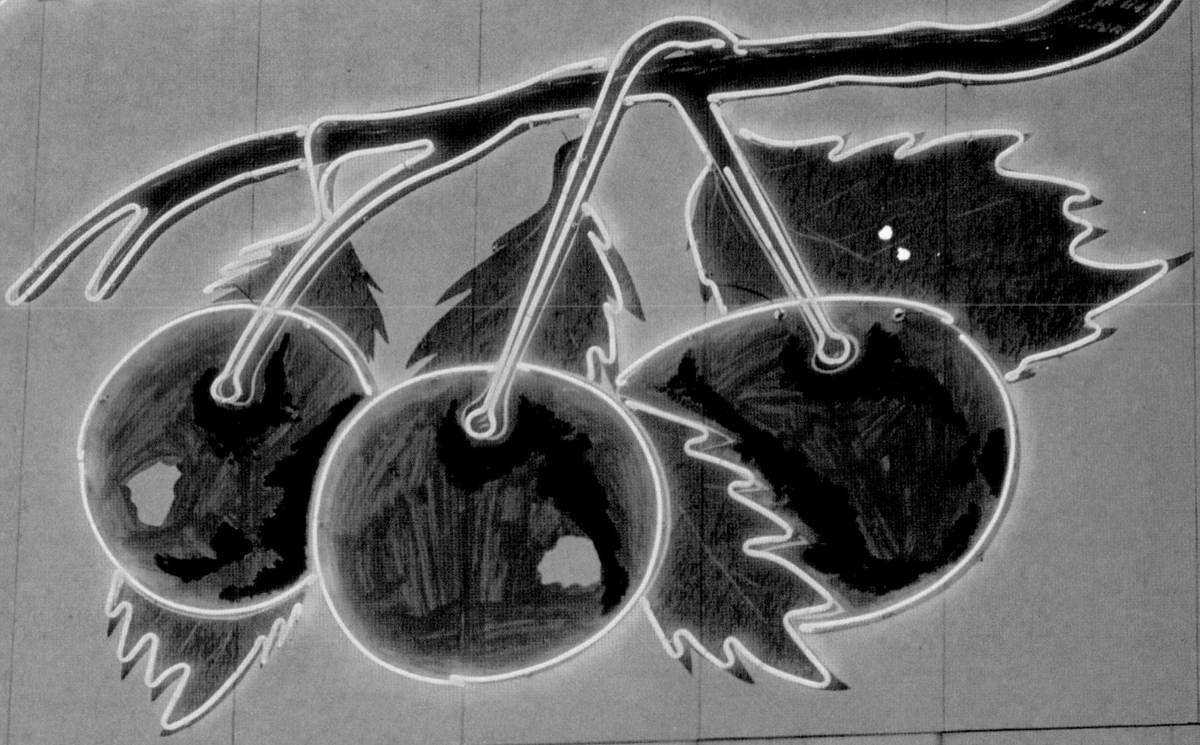
CHERRY BOMB®
BRAND FIRECRACKERS
SMOKING
OPEN
OUT
IN
GOOD HUMOR
GOOD HUMOR

© BUD LEE

© BUD LEE

▼ © DOROTHY B. JOHNSTON

▲ © DOROTHY B. JOHNSTON

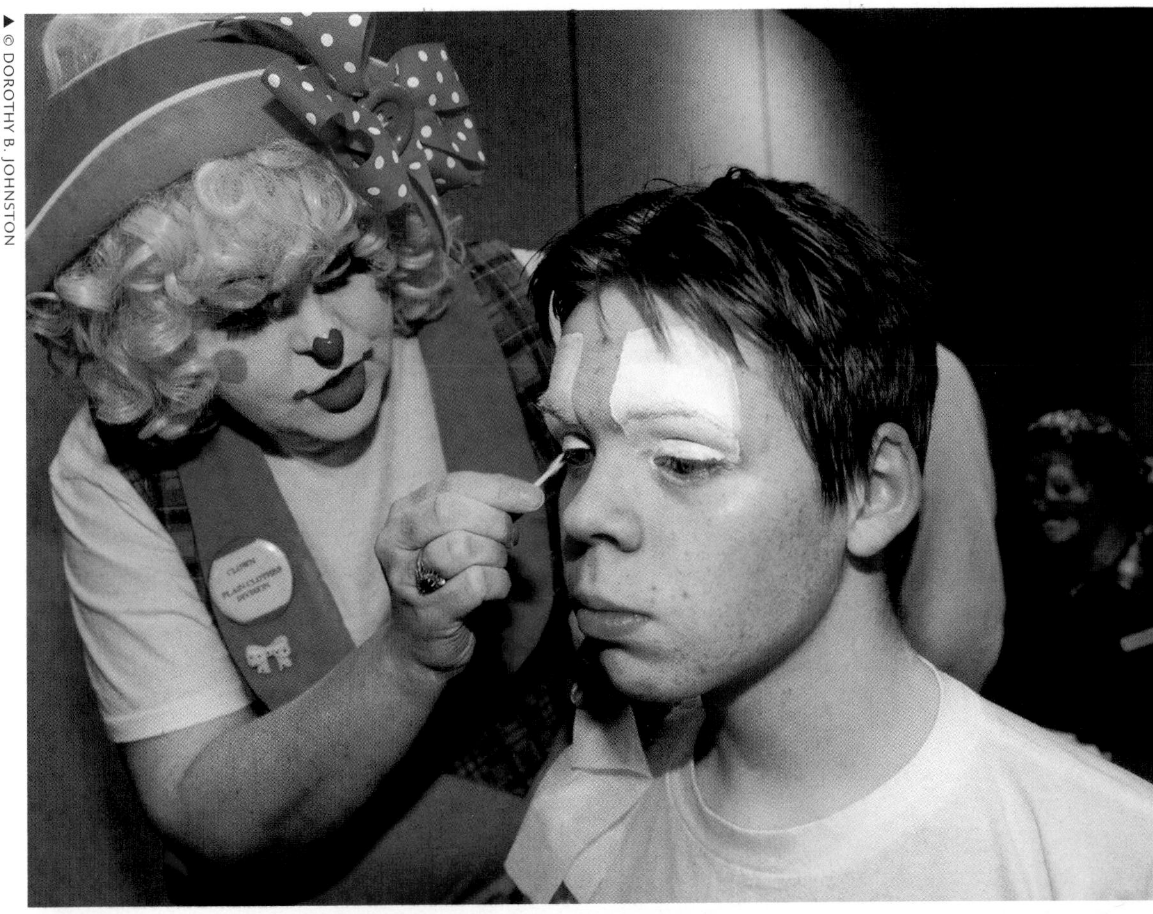

▲ © DOROTHY B. JOHNSTON

Making up is hard to do: A group of teachers from local Catholic schools participate in a makeover session at the Campbell County Extension Center (bottom), also the site of a separate event teaching participants a more theatrical form of face painting. Clowning around is the order of the day at a festival in Erlanger as well.

▼ © PAULA NORTON / NORTON PHOTOSTOCK

© PAULA NORTON / NORTON PHOTOSTOCK

Revelers from New Orleans have nothing on the celebrants from Covington when it comes time for the city's annual Mardi Gras festivities.

© DOROTHY B. JOHNSTON

© DOROTHY B. JOHNSTON

▶ © ANNE PINNAU

▶ © DOROTHY B. JOHNSTON

A WIDE VARIETY OF MUSICAL FARE is always on tap for Northern Kentucky listeners, from gospel and Latino to rock and jazz.

▼ © TOM UHLMAN

▼ © TOM UHLMAN

▶ © TOM UHLMAN

▶ © TOM UHLMAN

Northern Kentucky in silhouette casts an idyllic glow on the daily activities of the folks who call the region home.

▼ © CINCINNATI MUSEUM CENTER

▲ © MARK BOWEN / 2 GUYS AND SOME SLIDES

Florence is home to renowned Turfway Park, renamed and rejuvenated in 1986 from its earlier incarnation, historic Latonia Park (opposite). Today, the 200-acre facility conducts 105 days each year of Thoroughbred racing and is open year-round for simulcast wagering.

▲ © DOROTHY B. JOHNSTON

Northern Kentucky offers plenty of horsing around, whether it's for sport or for competition.

▼ © DOROTHY B. JOHNSTON

▼ © DOROTHY B. JOHNSTON

▼ © DOROTHY B. JOHNSTON

▲ © DOROTHY B. JOHNSTON

WHO SAID THIS WAS HORSE country? Whether pint-sized or pony-sized, man's best friend appears to rule the roost—at least on some days—in cities throughout Northern Kentucky.

▲ © DOROTHY B. JOHNSTON

▼ © DAN TYE

▲ © DOROTHY B. JOHNSTON

▲ © DOROTHY B. JOHNSTON

NORTHERN KENTUCKY HAS LONG had its share of role models for youngsters. Although born across the river in 1850, Daniel Carter Beard (OPPOSITE)—a founder of the Boy Scouts of America—grew up in Covington's Licking Historic District. Modern-day heroes also contribute to the region in a variety of ways.

© BEHRINGER-CRAWFORD MUSEUM

▸ © D.A. Brown / Behringer-Crawford Museum

The Behringer-Crawford Museum (above), located in Covington, exhibits and preserves the art and history of Northern Kentucky. The site of many annual events, including the Deutsche Familienfest (opposite bottom) and the holiday toy train display (opposite top), the museum is a groundbreaker in children's educational programming.

PEPSI
say "Pepsi, please"

© DALE VOELKER

© DALE VOELKER

UNSPOILED BY RAMPANT DEVELopment, the rural areas of Northern Kentucky reflect a simpler way of life.

© CARL E. SCHMITT

© WILLIAM V. WEST

▶ © DOROTHY B. JOHNSTON

To many, Kentucky is synonymous with tobacco. The state produces more than 4.5 million pounds of the leaf annually, generating some $8.5 million in sales.

FIVE BRIDGES SPAN THE OHIO River between Cincinnati and Kentucky, including the John A. Roebling Suspension Bridge, which provides a connection to Covington (BOTTOM). Built in 1866, the bridge is one of the area's architectural treasures.

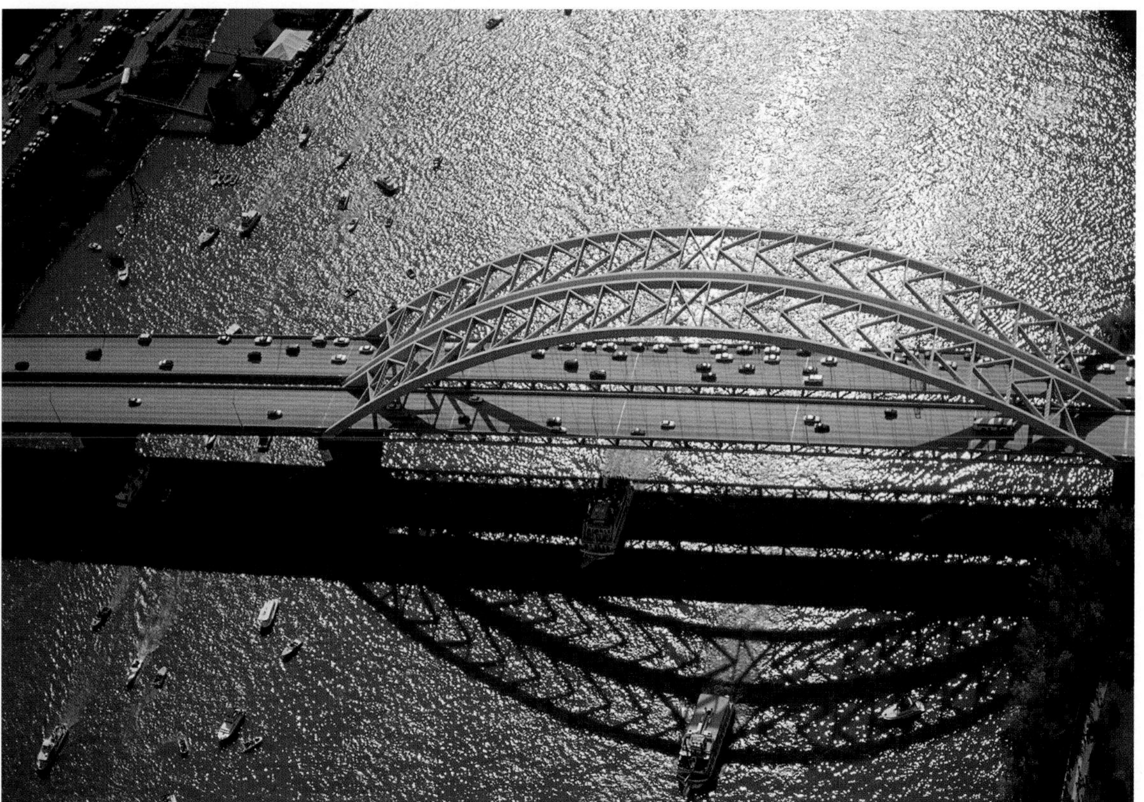

▲ © TOM UHLMAN

▲ © RICK NORTON / NORTON PHOTOSTOCK

▲ © MARY NEMETH

▲ © WILLARD CLAY / GEOIMAGERY

NORTHERN KENTUCKIANS WANTing to visit some beautiful natural treasures can travel to Daniel Boone National Forest in the east central part of the state for a day of outdoor adventure. Among the area's many sights are Sky Bridge (TOP) and the scenic Red River Gorge (BOTTOM).

BOONE. No 6

▶ © BUD LEE

▶ © BUD LEE

Anderson Ferry has connected Northern Kentucky to the western edge of Cincinnati since 1817. Listed on the National Register of Historic Places, it is one of only four ferries still in operation on the Ohio River today, and treats riders to a six-minute trip over a 700-yard stretch of the river.

▶ © BUD LEE

▶ © BUD LEE

▶ © BUD LEE

▶ © BUD LEE

▲ © MALCOM J. WILSON / NORTON PHOTOSTOCK

DEVASTATION STRUCK NORTHern Kentucky in the spring of 1997 when the Ohio River flooded its banks. Before the flood was over, the river had crested in Cincinnati at 64.7 feet—more than 12 feet above flood stage and nearly 40 feet higher than normal—making it the worst flood since 1964. Similar flooding proved problematic for area residents in 1937 (PAGES 88 AND 89).

▲ © RICK NORTON / NORTON PHOTOSTOCK

▼ © ROGER BICKEL

▼ © WILLIAM V. WEST

▲ © TOM UHLMAN

SINCE THE EARLY 1800S, THE mighty Ohio River has drawn industry and travelers to the banks of Covington and its Ohio neighbor across the way. To celebrate its history of steam boating, Cincinnati hosts the Tall Stacks festival (OPPOSITE TOP) every four years. Originating in 1988, the festival features nearly 20 riverboats and attracts hundreds of thousands of people over its five-day run.

▲ © CHRIS CONE

Coca-Cola
Pepsi-Cola
ATOMIC BAR
ATOMIC BAR
514
11

© DON McCLAIN / McNEIL COLLECTION

On July 10, 1937, the Rosedale number six (above) reached the end of its line. Beautiful but obsolete, the streetcar was retired to make way for a newer breed of public transportation—the gasoline-powered bus. Running lines from Cincinnati to Covington and Newport, the number six and other similar streetcars once provided the necessary link across the Ohio River.

▲ © ANNE PINNAU

DEDICATED IN 1901, COVINGTON'S spectacular Cathedral Basilica of the Assumption (OPPOSITE) is modeled after the Gothic Abbey Church of Saint-Denis, near Paris, and Notre Dame. Equally historic, though smaller in scale, the Monte Casino Chapel on the campus of Thomas More College in Crestview Hills is believed to be the world's tiniest place of worship.

ROBERT J. KLING
COUNTY CLERK
AUTOMOBILE DEPT.
NO
PARKING
BUS
STOP

▲ © KEITH D. YOUTCHEFF PHOTOGRAPHY

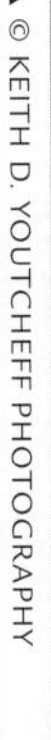

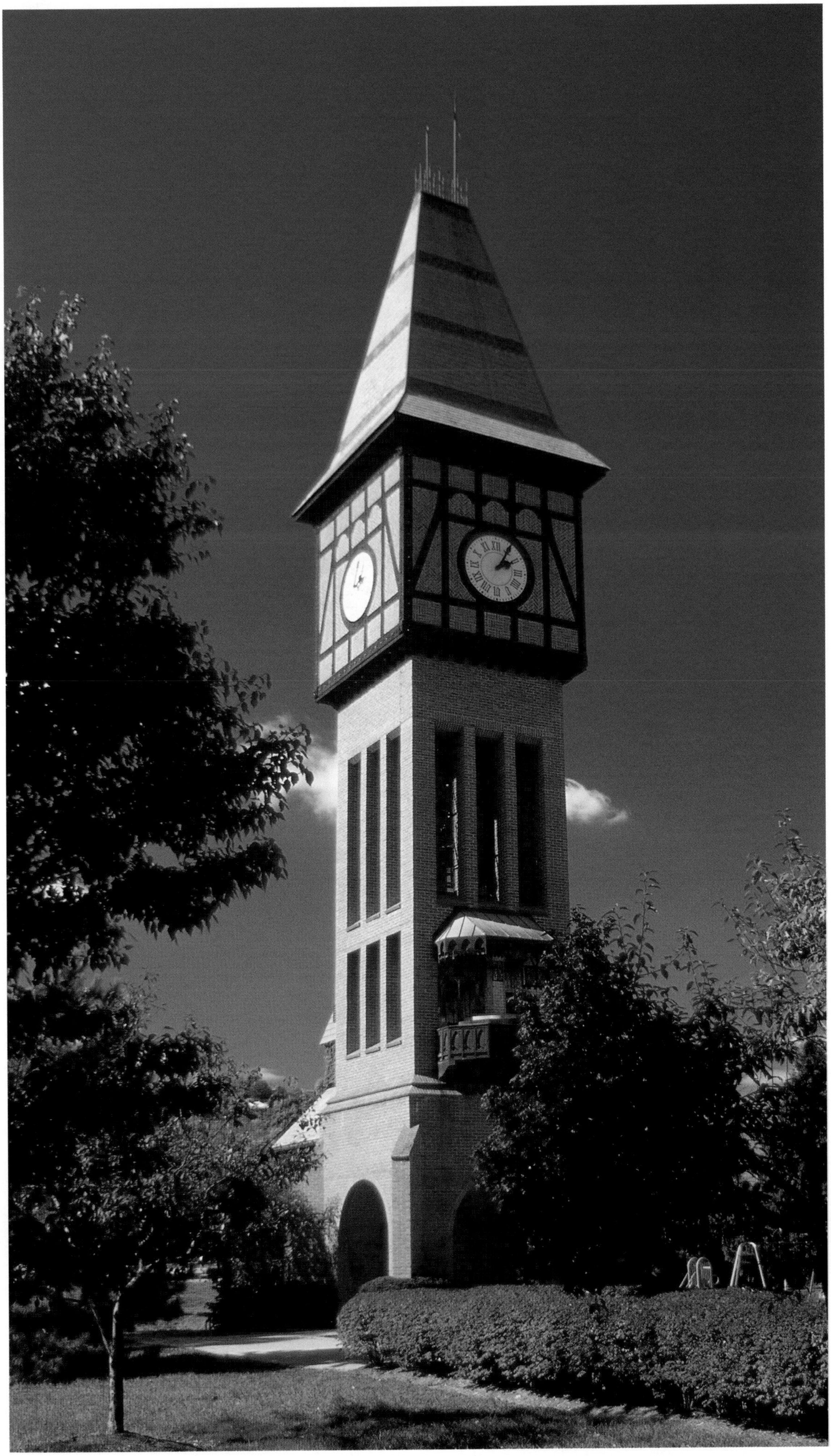

HISTORIC CAMPBELL COUNTY Courthouse in Newport (OPPOSITE) was built in 1884, designed in Queen Anne style with stained glass windows and a marble staircase. Covington's Goebel Park is home to the Carroll Chimes Bell Tower, built in 1979 and named in honor of then Governor Julian Carroll. The German Gothic tower houses a 43-bell glockenspiel that chimes each hour, and features 21 mechanical figures that enact the German fairy tale of the Pied Piper of Hamelin.

▼ © DOROTHY B. JOHNSTON

▼ © DOROTHY B. JOHNSTON

▼ © DOROTHY B. JOHNSTON

▶ © DOROTHY B. JOHNSTON

On June 20, 1999, the seven-story Campbell Towers office building—the tallest structure in Newport—was imploded. The demolition makes way for the planned Millennium Monument project, which will include a pavilion containing its centerpiece, the World Peace Bell, said to be the world's largest swinging bell.

▶ © DOROTHY B. JOHNSTON

▶ © DOROTHY B. JOHNSTON

© CINCINNATI MUSEUM CENTER

© TOM UHLMAN

© DOROTHY B. JOHNSTON

© DOROTHY B. JOHNSTON

© TOM UHLMAN

A HIGHLY MOBILE WORKFORCE that is drawn from both Northern Kentucky and Cincinnati has helped to make the Tri-County area a mecca for the steel industry. Companies like Newport Steel (OPPOSITE) have been part of the local landscape since the 1880s.

◆ © DALE VOELKER

BUSINESS DEVELOPMENT IN Northern Kentucky has been booming during the past decade, giving rise to buildings such as Newport's One Riverfront Place (OPPOSITE) and Covington's RiverCenter Towers, an office/hotel complex.

▲ © MARK BOWEN / 2 GUYS AND SOME SLIDES

▲ © DOROTHY B. JOHNSTON

▶ © CINCINNATI MUSEUM CENTER

THE FINANCIAL INDUSTRY HAS long been a mainstay of Northern Kentucky's business community, from the earliest days at First Federal Savings and Loan in Covington (ABOVE) to more recent times at the offices of the Internal Revenue Service.

© DOROTHY B. JOHNSTON

© DOROTHY B. JOHNSTON

▲ © BUD LEE

A quality education is at the core of efforts to make Northern Kentucky a great place to call home.

▼ © DOROTHY B. JOHNSTON

▼ © DOROTHY B. JOHNSTON

▲ © DOROTHY B. JOHNSTON

SCHOLARSHIP CERTAINLY HAS ITS rewards, and movin' on up—via graduation—is just one of them.

▼ © MARK BOWEN / 2 GUYS AND SOME SLIDES

▼ © DOROTHY B. JOHNSTON

▼ © DOROTHY B. JOHNSTON

© MARK BOWEN / 2 GUYS AND SOME SLIDES

© DOROTHY B. JOHNSTON

Among the array of athletic and fitness events Northern Kentucky has to offer is the annual Jingle Bell Run for Arthritis (opposite top), a five-kilometer race where some runners get into the holiday spirit by wearing fake antlers along the course.

© MARK BOWEN / 2 GUYS AND SOME SLIDES

© MARK BOWEN / 2 GUYS AND SOME SLIDES

© MARK BOWEN / 2 GUYS AND SOME SLIDES

▲ © STEPHEN DUNN / ALLSPORT USA

▲ © DOUG PENSINGER / ALLSPORT USA

THE NFL'S CINCINNATI BENGALS have big plans to move into Paul Brown Stadium at the start of the 2000 football season. Meanwhile, the team remains a fixture at Cinergy Field—formerly known as Riverfront Stadium—drawing thousands of die-hard fans to their home games.

© BRIAN BAHR / ALLSPORT USA

© MATTHEW STOCKMAN / ALLSPORT USA

© JED JACOBSOHN / ALLSPORT USA

Although game attire was a bit more formal in 1909 (above), take me out to the ballgame has long been a rallying cry for fans of the Cincinnati Reds. During the 1970s, the Big Red Machine rolled over its opponents, racking up six division titles, four National League pennants, and two World Series titles with back-to-back wins in 1975 and 1976. These days, pitcher Denny Neagle (opposite top) and infielders Barry Larkin (opposite, bottom left) and Pokey Reese (opposite, bottom right) are helping return the team to its winning ways.

▼ © DOROTHY B. JOHNSTON

▼ © DOROTHY B. JOHNSTON

▲ © DOROTHY B. JOHNSTON

IN NORTHERN KENTUCKY, IT'S OK to blow your own horn—or flute—especially when the occasion calls for celebration and ceremony.

▲ © DOROTHY B. JOHNSTON

▲ © MARK BOWEN / 2 GUYS AND SOME SLIDES

THE CARNEGIE

▲ © BUD LEE

▲ © BUD LEE

Since 1975, the Carnegie Arts Center (opposite) has been ground zero for the burgeoning Northern Kentucky arts scene. Built in 1904, the beaux arts building was originally one of the first Carnegie Foundation-funded libraries in the country, and today is a place for emerging artists to exhibit visual art and perform original plays.

▶ © JANE GAHL

▶ © DAN TYE

THE HISTORIC CATHEDRAL Basilica of the Assumption in Covington has many glorious architectural features, but perhaps its greatest is the abundance of stained glass that frames its walls. The sanctuary features the world's largest handblown stained glass window.

▲ © DOROTHY B. JOHNSTON

▲ © MARK BOWEN / 2 GUYS AND SOME SLIDES

▲ © MARK BOWEN / 2 GUYS AND SOME SLIDES

▲ © DOROTHY B. JOHNSTON

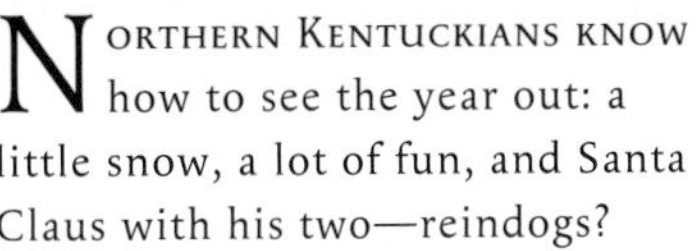

Northern Kentuckians know how to see the year out: a little snow, a lot of fun, and Santa Claus with his two—reindogs? However area residents choose to honor the passage of time, paying tribute to the rich history and bright future of Boone, Campbell, and Kenton counties is indeed a worthy way to look to the new millennium.

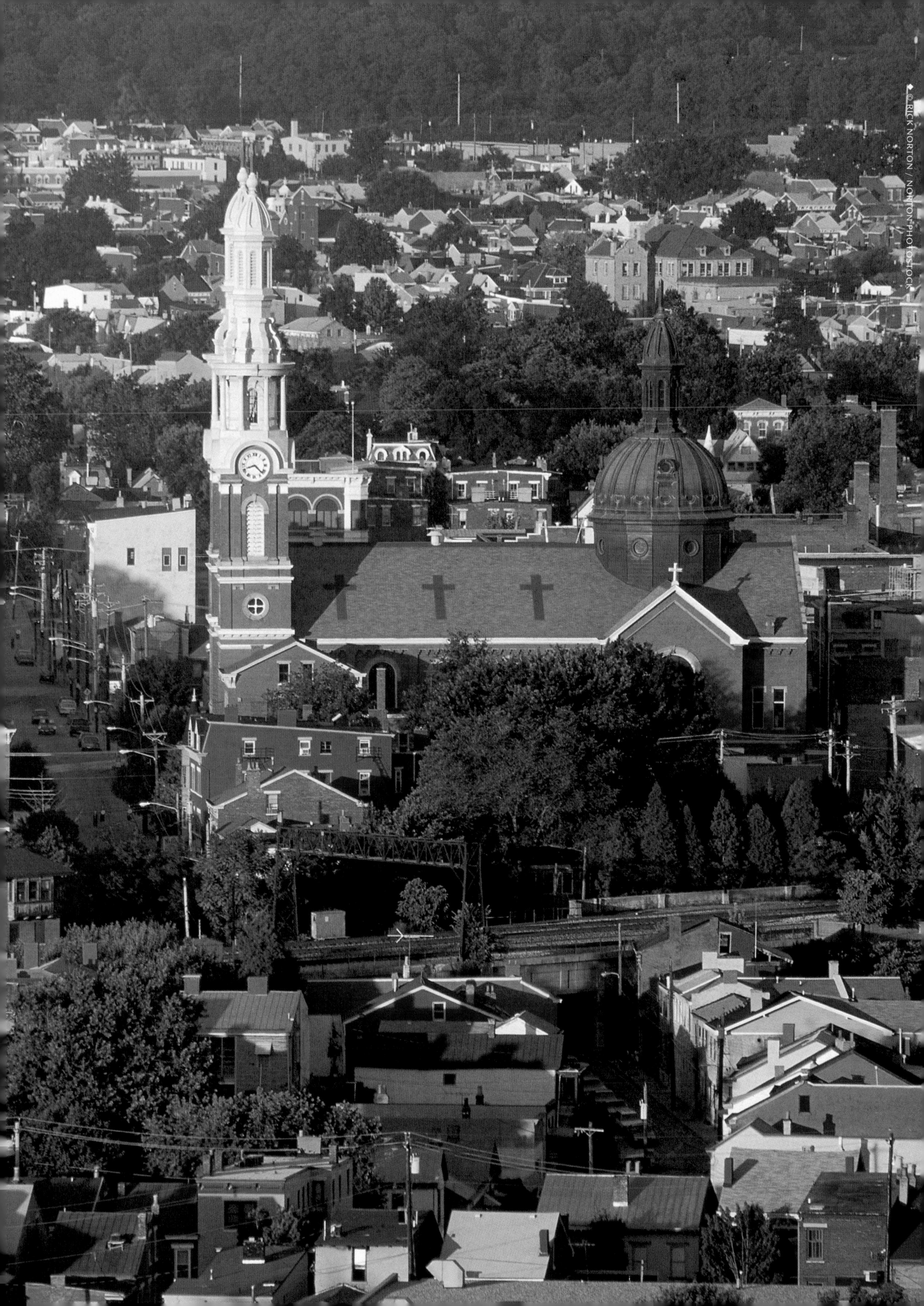

PROFILES IN EXCELLENCE

A look at the corporations, businesses, professional groups, and community service organizations that have made this book possible. Their stories—offering an informal chronicle of the local business community—are arranged according to the date they were established in Northern Kentucky.

■ Ashland Inc. ■ Baptist Life Communities ■ Business Benefits, Inc. ■ CenterBrain International, Inc. ■ Cincinnati Children's Hospital Medical Center ■ The Cincinnati Gear Company ■ City of Covington ■ City of Newport ■ Comair, Inc. ■ David E. Estes Engineering, Inc. ■ Dixie Chili & Deli ■ Drawbridge Estate ■ The Drees Company ■ GBBN Architects ■ GE Capital IT Solutions ■ Holland Roofing Group ■ Littleford Day, Inc. ■ Louis Trauth Dairy, Inc. ■ MacKay, Inc. ■ Maxfield, Schwartz, Lonnemann & Kohrs, PSC ■ The Northern Kentucky Symphony ■ Northern Kentucky Convention Center Corporation ■ Northern Kentucky Chamber of Commerce ■ Northern Kentucky Convention & Visitors Bureau ■ NS Group, Inc. ■ Rumpke Consolidated Companies, Inc. ■ SpanPro, Inc. ■ Spartan Construction ■ St. Elizabeth Medical Center ■ The St. Luke Hospitals ■ TENTE CASTERS, Inc. ■ Toyota Motor Manufacturing North America, Inc. (TMMNA) ■ Tri-County Economic Development Corporation of Northern Kentucky ■ WCPO-TV ■ WILD Flavors, Inc. ■ Willamette Industries Preprint Plant ■ WNKR Mix 106.5 FM ■ xpedx ■

1775-1949

1775 City of Newport

1815 City of Covington

1861 St. Elizabeth Medical Center

1882 Littleford Day, Inc.

1883 Cincinnati Children's Hospital Medical Center

1907 The Cincinnati Gear Company

1919 xpedx

1920 Louis Trauth Dairy, Inc.

1928 The Drees Company

1929 Dixie Chili & Deli

1932 Rumpke Consolidated Companies, Inc.

1949 WCPO-TV

N MAY 19, 1775, A GROUP OF EXPLORERS FROM ENGLAND AND *Virginia paddled past the future site of Dayton, Kentucky, and disembarked at the terminus of the Licking River, where its waters merged with the mighty Ohio. Among this party of adventurers and surveyors was Captain Edmund Taylor of Orange County, Virginia, who would spread the word about the rich lands and* wondrous woods to be found at the confluence of the two great rivers. Indeed, his cousin James Taylor—who later gained notoriety as a military general—helped found what would eventually become the City of Newport.

J. MILES WOLF

City of Growth

On the eve of America's quest for independence, the founders of Newport established a unique community amid verdant surroundings—rich with good soil, ample forests, and room to grow. From its genesis more than 200 years ago, Newport has experienced a wide spectrum of development and growth, even overcoming a period of adversity when it was known as Sin City. But more than anything, this community, bordered on the west by the Licking River and on the north by the Ohio, has grown to become a vibrant, important keystone of the Greater Cincinnati region.

Blessed with some of Kentucky's largest historic districts, Newport looks forward to a new millennium with a keen sense of its character and potential. Newport is experiencing tremendous economic growth, with more than $300 million in development projects on the table, and anticipates even more in the near future. With its can-do attitude, the city has become a role model for other small communities throughout the Commonwealth.

The City of Newport has gained a reputation as a go-getter when it comes to development and forward-looking projects. It is home to the privately developed, state-of-the-art Oceanic Adventures Newport Aquarium, the anchor attraction for the Newport on the Levee riverfront entertainment destination center. The city has also scored its share of accolades when it comes to attracting major businesses to town, including such international firms as Heinz Pet Products, Star-Kist Foods, and Sencorp.

According to city leaders, it is important to look carefully at all new development in the context of Newport's rich history. Its East Row Historic District, the second-largest local historic district in the state of Kentucky, contains some of the most beautiful vintage Queen Anne-style row houses in the country, and reflects the city's importance as home to many generations of Kentuckians. The preserved commercial buildings in the Monmouth Street Historic District

CLOCKWISE FROM TOP:
THE CITY OF NEWPORT HAS GAINED A REPUTATION AS A GO-GETTER WHEN IT COMES TO DEVELOPMENT AND FORWARD-LOOKING PROJECTS, SUCH AS RIVERBOAT ROW.

FROM ITS GENESIS MORE THAN 200 YEARS AGO, THE CITY HAS EXPERIENCED A WIDE SPECTRUM OF DEVELOPMENT AND GROWTH.

BORDERED ON THE WEST BY THE LICKING RIVER AND ON THE NORTH BY THE OHIO, NEWPORT HAS GROWN TO BECOME A VIBRANT, IMPORTANT KEYSTONE OF THE GREATER CINCINNATI REGION.

J. MILES WOLF

▼▲ J. MILES WOLF

DURING THE 1950S, THE STOREFRONTS ALONG MONMOUTH STREET PROVIDED SHOPPERS WITH A VARIETY OF GOODS AND SERVICES. TODAY, THE CITY OF NEWPORT HAS USED THE PRESERVATION OF THESE HISTORIC BUILDINGS AND NEIGHBORHOODS AS AN ECONOMIC DEVELOPMENT TOOL.

trace the development of Campbell County's original Main Street. The City of Newport has used the preservation of its historic buildings and neighborhoods as an economic development tool. For example, any exterior alterations within either the East Row or Monmouth Street historic districts must conform with design review guidelines in order to preserve the historic integrity of these areas, thus maintaining their desirability.

Confronting Challenges

Despite its current level of prosperity, Newport has faced its share of struggles in years past, confronting a range of challenges common to older, urbanized regions. Situated adjacent to Covington and Cincinnati, it is a relatively small city, totaling approximately 18,800 people within three square miles. The population was at its peak of 31,000 residents during the 1950s, and Monmouth Street's storefronts provided shoppers with a variety of goods and services. In the years that followed, industries shut down, families moved to the suburbs, and businesses closed. That situation left Newport with many challenges.

Among the issues Newport has addressed in recent years was determining how to balance serving an aging population, providing high quality services to residents, preserving the rich variety of architecture within the city limits, and attracting new businesses to this community surrounded by other cities and regions competing for the same prospects and moneys. A professional and persistent city staff, functioning as a team, has generated the recent high level of activity seen in the city today.

Another source of Newport's strength is its stability with regard to elected officials. "We are fortunate to have a stable government," states Phil Ciafardini, Newport city manager. "Our mayor and city commissioners work very well together because it is always the greater good of the city that they keep as their goal. Because of that, they are able to get things done." Reflective of this goal is the state and national accreditation attained by the Newport Police Department and the advanced life support services provided by the fire department.

The small-town charm of Newport is never more evident than during its many local festivals. Celebrating the city's rich Italian heritage is the Festa Italiana, a four-day event featuring authentic Italian food, performers, and even an opera with symphonic accompaniment. The Newport Arts and Music Festival highlights the talents of local artists and musicians, while the Kentucky State Championship Chili Cook-Off and Car Show features the hottest cars and chili in the region. The annual events culminate with one of the top 10 holiday events in the state, the Victorian Christmas Tour. Held in the East Row Historic District, the tour highlights the Victorian era homes dressed up in their holiday finest.

As it looks toward the new millennium, the City of Newport reflects on its long list of accomplishments while constantly weighing its goals for the future. "We are continuing to work to stabilize our neighborhoods, to revitalize our downtown, and to improve the quality of life in Newport," Ciafardini says. "We have made great strides in the past 17 years, but there is still much to do."

VER THE PAST DECADE, COVINGTON HAS EMERGED AS THE *center of an explosion of commercial and cultural revitalization across Northern Kentucky. Demographically, Covington is the largest and wealthiest municipality in the area. Geographically, it is the most centralized, and the city lies directly across the historic John A. Roebling Suspension Bridge from downtown Cincinnati.*

Economically, Covington is home to the area's most dynamic companies, the biggest recent construction projects, and the top hotels, restaurants, and nightspots.

Incorporated in 1815, the city is an ideal blend of old and new. With 15 national historic districts (more than any other city in the region, including Cincinnati), Covington's numerous neighborhoods and business centers combine big-city convenience with small-town, turn-of-the-century ambience. Licking Riverside, MainStrasse Village, Wallace Woods, and the downtown business core are among the historical districts, and notable historic buildings include the Cathedral Basilica of the Assumption, the twin-spired Mother of God Church, the Carnegie Arts Center, and the former Bavarian Brewery (now Jillian's).

Attracting Corporate Citizens

Even as it preserves its rich heritage, Covington is attracting a flurry of new construction to accommodate burgeoning business, commercial, and governmental activities. Unlike so many other cities, Covington has not made a habit of tearing down its past, so until recently, it had relatively little developable land to attract new projects. However, revitalization along the Ohio River has cleared out former industrial land that is now suitable for new commercial enterprises. Meanwhile, land in the southern parts of the city has been opened up by Interstate 275. The RiverCenter complex, new federal and county courthouses, several new national chain hotels, the Northern Kentucky Convention Center, and Fidelity Investments' Magellan office campus are all direct results of that process.

Covington's riverfront skyline, accentuated by the RiverCenter office towers, is in many ways a symbol of the transformation that is taking place citywide, as corporations continue to flock to town. Jacor Communications, Gibson Greetings, and Omnicare all left Cincinnati to relocate south of the river in Covington. Spurning lucrative offers from out of state, Ashland Inc. picked Covington for its new corporate headquarters when the Kentucky company decided to pull up stakes in its namesake hometown. Fidelity Investments and GE Capital also chose the city for major division headquarters and operations that relocated from out of state. They now employ thousands of local residents.

One surefire measure of Covington's success in attracting corporate residents is the number and quality of new hotels that have sprung up, largely to accommodate business travelers from around the globe. City officials like to point out that when the governor visited Northern Kentucky in the past, he stayed overnight at a hotel in Cincinnati. Now, when the governor (or the president of the United States, for that matter)

◀ RICK NORTON/NORTON PHOTOSTOCK

GEOGRAPHICALLY, COVINGTON IS THE MOST CENTRALIZED CITY IN NORTHERN KENTUCKY, AND IT LIES DIRECTLY ACROSS THE HISTORIC JOHN A. ROEBLING SUSPENSION BRIDGE FROM DOWNTOWN CINCINNATI.

RICK NORTON/NORTON PHOTOSTOCK

comes to the area, he stays in Covington—because that's where the best rooms are.

At Home in Covington

The city's downtown business district has also been transformed by the changing times. Formerly Northern Kentucky's principal shopping district, the area's role as a retail center has been usurped by suburban malls and power centers. Lately, however, downtown Covington has been enjoying a renaissance, as professionals and other service businesses have discovered that it is an ideal office location. Convenient to RiverCenter and downtown Cincinnati, Covington's central business district affords quick access to all of the area's major highways. Best of all, downtown offices cost a fraction of what other nearby high-rise suites go for these days. As businesses see the value and the advantages the city has to offer, so too do many of their employees. Rather than commuting an hour or more every day in traffic, workers who choose to settle in Covington can enjoy breathtaking river views and will be within walking distance of RiverCenter, downtown Cincinnati, and the entire waterfront on either side of the Ohio. Covington offers affordable living, an eclectic mix of new and old housing stock, hundreds of shops and restaurants, tree-lined residential streets, convenient highway connections, and close proximity to the Cincinnati/Northern Kentucky International Airport.

Of course, modern living isn't complete without golf, and it just so happens that the two closest courses to downtown Cincinnati are both in Covington. The scenic Devou Park Golf Course offers panoramic views of the entire valley, while the cozy Twin Oaks Golf Course welcomes players along the banks of the Licking River. Both are regulation 18-hole courses that are open to the public and are within a 10-minute drive of RiverCenter.

If walking or driving isn't a convenient way to get around Covington, there is also a shuttle bus that runs a 20-minute loop in both directions from MainStrasse Village to downtown Cincinnati and all along the Northern Kentucky riverfront. Connecting bustling entertainment and shopping districts in Covington, Newport, and Bellevue, the 25-cent shuttles run continuously every day.

Still at the very heart of Northern Kentucky as it enters the 21st century, Covington has preserved the very best of the old while attracting more than its share of the new. As many residents enthusiastically profess, it's a great place to work and a great place to live—all within a few blocks.

INCORPORATED IN 1815, COVINGTON IS AN IDEAL BLEND OF OLD AND NEW. WITH 15 NATIONAL HISTORIC DISTRICTS, ITS NUMEROUS NEIGHBORHOODS AND BUSINESS CENTERS COMBINE BIG-CITY CONVENIENCE WITH SMALL-TOWN, TURN-OF-THE-CENTURY AMBIENCE.

As John A. Roebling was overseeing the construction *of his famous suspension bridge across the Ohio River in Covington, Kentucky, the area's first health care facility was being opened by the Franciscan Sisters of the Poor at the urging of Covington's Catholic Bishop George A. Carrell. Since its austere genesis in a small, three-story, remodeled grocery store* on 7th Street between Madison and Scott streets, St. Elizabeth has grown into one of the region's most respected medical centers, providing the full spectrum of health care in its North Unit in Covington, its sprawling South Unit in Edgewood, and its Grant County Unit in Williamstown.

Delivering Quality Care

The past two decades have transformed St. Elizabeth into a system that continues to expand to meet the needs of the growing Northern Kentucky community. Throughout the 1990s, the medical center not only dramatically broadened the range of services it offers, but followed a clear strategic direction in redefining itself into an integrated health system. Through this period, the medical center enjoyed an impressive increase in market share, community image, and patient satisfaction, while maintaining its place as one of the area's lowest cost providers and attracting the highest managed care penetration enjoyed by any local hospital.

Along with growth in services and facilities, the late 1990s brought St. Elizabeth prestigious recognition as a superior regional medical center and an active force in the improvement of area health care. A banner year, 1998 started with the announcement that St. Elizabeth had been ranked among the nation's 100 top cost-effective, high-quality hospitals. Underscoring this achievement was the welcome news that St. Elizabeth had achieved highest overall scores among all major hospitals in both Ohio and Kentucky in a major insurer's quality studies.

Today, St. Elizabeth is one of the largest acute-care hospitals in Kentucky, treating nearly 22,000 inpatients, 275,000 outpatients, and more than 87,000 emergency patients annually. The center's 2,900 employees make it one of the largest employers in Northern Kentucky.

A Full-Service Hospital System

The St. Elizabeth System's two main facilities—the North Unit in Covington and the South Unit in Edgewood—are both full-service hospitals, with medical-surgical and critical-care beds, emergency and outpatient facilities, and modern diagnostic and treatment services.

The North Unit has an inpatient and outpatient kidney dialysis program, a sleep disorders center, a skilled/extended-care nursing unit, an inpatient and outpatient hospice program, a home care agency, and a medical office building.

The South Unit, which opened in 1978, has continually been the growth engine of the group. It includes a Family Practice Residency program, two medical office buildings, pediatric services, a birthing center, a special care unit for newborns, a sports medicine center, a center for women's wellness, spe-

The North Unit chapel is a beautiful setting for prayer and reflection (right).

More than 145 physicians have graduated from the St. Elizabeth Family Practice Residency Program (left).

cialized cancer treatment services, comprehensive behavioral health services, rehabilitation services, and a business health program. St. Elizabeth's cardiac program, based at the South Unit, has become one of the most highly regarded services in the Midwest for the diagnosis and treatment of heart disease. The program is acclaimed for outstanding care and risk-adjusted patient mortality rates far below national averages both for noninvasive cardiac procedures as well as for open-heart surgery.

The third facility affiliated with St. Elizabeth Medical Center, the former Grant County Hospital, is a 30-bed community hospital in Williamstown that offers acute inpatient care, emergency care, and outpatient services. Local patients in need of outpatient testing now benefit from newly acquired technology, such as a CT scanner, fluoroscopy, and other diagnostic radiography procedures.

Sponsored by the Diocese of Covington, St. Elizabeth joined Catholic Healthcare Partners (CHP) of Cincinnati in 1998. This membership makes the Northern Kentucky hospital group the 10th region for CHP, which is the largest health care system in Ohio and the seventh-largest nonprofit system in the United States.

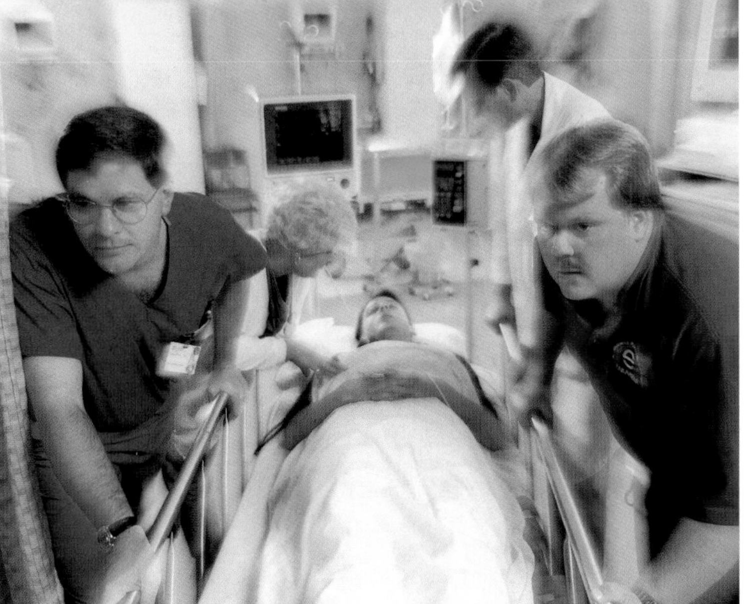

Clockwise from top left: St. Elizabeth Grant County offers a wide array of outpatient services, including a medical laboratory.

The beautiful birthing rooms and experienced staff at the Family Birth Place give Northern Kentucky babies a great start.

The emergency departments in Covington, Edgewood, and Grant County care for more than 87,000 patients a year.

A Living Responsibility

At St. Elizabeth, the hospital's mission isn't an abstract philosophy—it's a living responsibility, "to deliver quality, personalized care and services and, within our capabilities, to treat all persons in the Northern Kentucky area who need health services but cannot afford the cost," says CEO Joe Gross. Far from being just rhetoric, St. Elizabeth's board of trustees, administration, staff, and supporters are fully committed to the medical center's mission of care. This was a primary reason for the 1990 formation of a foundation to support the advancement of hospital and indigent care causes. Over 100 volunteer community leaders make up the foundation and actively champion the role of the medical center in the community. Hospital employees are strongly dedicated to the medical center as well, with a low employee turnover rate despite a thriving Northern Kentucky job market. More remarkably, the hospital's employee-organized VISION participation program, which encourages contributions from associates, has raised more than $1.5 million through four campaigns and has become a model other hospitals aspire to match.

"When you think about St. Elizabeth Medical Center, you have to think beyond the walls," says Gross. "We deliver health care where people need it, when they need it. We also provide millions of dollars every year in care to the poor. Last year alone, we spent close to $10 million for indigent care."

This dedication to quality and comprehensive care, available to all who need it, has been a tradition at the hospital since its founding more than a century ago, and will continue to guide St. Elizabeth Medical Center into the next millennium.

INCE ITS FOUNDING IN 1882, LITTLEFORD DAY, INC. HAS EVOLVED *into one of the Tri-State's most innovative manufacturing companies. According to Littleford Day President Donald Steedman, the Northern Kentucky-based firm has had a long history of adapting to the changing demands of the marketplace and its clients. World renowned for its advanced drying technology and state-of-the-art* mixing technology for the chemical, food, pharmaceutical, plastic, and many other industries, Littleford Day is today a model for companies looking to adapt to the changing demands of customers and the times.

A History of Change

Founded in the 19th century by John Littleford, who arrived in the Queen City from England, Littleford Bros.—as it was eventually called—started out as a job shop in the steel fabrication business, with a plant located near the foot of Pearl Street in Cincinnati, by the Ohio River. From that beginning, Littleford Day developed two primary product lines: a complete array of equipment for the brewing industry, and proprietary equipment for asphalt road construction.

"Littleford made everything imaginable out of steel for all the early Cincinnati industries, including fabricated parts for riverboats; fabricated tubs and tanks for the early brewing industry, as well as the city's early soap industry; plus fabrication of ductwork and smokestacks for the nearby utilities—really everything that was going on at the time," Steedman says. Brewers for hundreds of miles around Cincinnati relied on Littleford Bros. to supply them with literally all their production equipment needs. After Prohibition shut down the brewing equipment business, Littleford honed its position as a leader in manufacturing asphalt road sprayer distributors, soil compaction equipment, paving equipment, and other asphalt equipment.

As Steedman notes, times and the demands on industry change, and so did the customer base for Littleford. The U.S. interstate highway system was being built with concrete rather than asphalt. So, in 1960, Littleford obtained a license from a German mixing company to manufacture newly developed mixing machines for

MANY EVERYDAY, HOUSEHOLD PRODUCTS ARE MADE USING MIXERS, DRYERS, AND REACTORS PRODUCED BY LITTLEFORD DAY, INC., INCLUDING THE SANITARY BATCH MIXER FOR MANUFACTURING NUTRITIONAL FOOD SUPPLEMENTS FOR CONSUMERS AND HOSPITALS (TOP); A BATCH REACTOR FOR MAKING THICKENERS FOR SALAD DRESSINGS, ICE CREAMS, AND OTHER FOODS (BOTTOM RIGHT); AND A SANITARY BATCH MIXER FOR MANUFACTURING INFANT MILK REPLACEMENT PRODUCTS (BOTTOM LEFT).

industrial process applications. Thus, Littleford's mixer division began. Motivated by its growth in the mixer business, the company in 1976 moved its headquarters and manufacturing operations to Florence, Kentucky. Littleford's concentration in developing mixing process technology and meeting the expanding needs of its customers eventually evolved into the company's other milieu—advanced drying technology.

Entering that field further allowed Littleford to adapt its mixer license to even more applications within a tremendous spectrum of industries, and enabled the firm to grow market share and increase sales. It also helped Littleford Day develop a broad-based platform for growth, in which it could look at many industries and pursue new niches as they evolved for its product lines.

In 1981, Littleford Bros. acquired the Day Mixing Division of LeBlond, Inc., in Norwood, Ohio, as a wholly owned subsidiary and renamed it the J.H. Day Company. The acquisition brought the firm many new products and, even more important, substantial growth. Operations of J.H. Day and Littleford were merged into Littleford's facilities in Florence, and the company became known as Littleford Day, Inc. in 1992.

Meeting Clients' Needs

Companies come to Littleford Day to seek solutions for their mixing, drying, and reacting process problems, and for development of new products and technologies. Today, Littleford Day serves clients such as Dow Chemical, Procter & Gamble, the Kroger Company, Duracell, Xerox, General Motors, General Foods, and the Kellogg Company, among dozens of other Fortune 500 companies, as well as numerous small entrepreneurs.

Utilizing its unique process development and testing program, Littleford Day helps its customers turn processing ideas into reality, and the company provides solutions along the way. In fact, Littleford Day's logo statement matches its endeavors: "Where processing ideas become reality."

"We are fully vertically integrated in our business processes," says Steedman. "We execute all design, engineering, and manufacturing operations here at our Florence facility. Our factory is fully equipped with modern CNC equipment, as well as our own proprietary production equipment.

"One of the things that has made us successful is the fact that we participate in the leading edge of our customers' technological developments," Steedman adds. "Not only do we work together as a business partner, but we actually assist them in developing new technologies so they can achieve and remain in the forefront of their markets."

Customers approach Littleford Day with the knowledge that its engineers, chemists, and process technicians will ultimately provide the solutions that only can be found at this innovative firm. On any given day, visitors at Littleford Day will discover customers working with the Littleford experts in identifying processes and creating new developments to meet the customer's needs. Visitors also can see the wide variety of equipment being manufactured at the Florence Industrial Park facility, from huge drying machines to elaborate, highly polished sanitary industrial mixers used in the pharmaceutical industry.

Still a family-owned company, Littleford Day strives to be more than just a business endeavor—the Littleford family has continuously reinvested profits from the business for the benefit of both customers and employees. "Littleford Day is an excellent place to work," Steedman says. "Not only have we become known for our advanced technology, but we are also recognized as one of the best places to work in the Tri-State. We have worked hard at creating the right environment that allows employees to grow, and it shows in the long-term employees we have here."

Utilizing its unique process development and testing program, Littleford Day produces mixers, dryers, and reactors that help its customers turn processing ideas into reality. Such products include a batch mixer for producing bulk molding compound in the manufacture of bathroom and kitchen sinks (top left); a continuous mixer for the production of household laundry detergents and automatic dishwasher detergents (top right); and a vacuum dryer for manufacture of metal powders to be used in machine tool parts (bottom).

Cincinnati Children's Hospital Medical Center

HEN CHILDREN NEED SPECIALIZED MEDICAL CARE—SUCH AS LIVER *or stem cell transplants—they come to Cincinnati Children's Hospital Medical Center. "The hospital may be best known as a place to provide sophisticated, high-tech care for very complex illnesses, but it also provides care across the entire spectrum, including well-child care, pediatric primary care, and rehabilitative and home care* services," says President and CEO James Anderson. "Our mission also emphasizes providing research and teaching programs that ensure delivery of the highest-quality pediatric care to our community, the nation, and the world."

As the only pediatric hospital in Greater Cincinnati, Cincinnati Children's is an advocate for children and provides care regardless of a family's ability to pay. "We provide a variety of medical, social, and financial services that are often unexpected in a hospital," Anderson says.

According to the National Association of Children's Hospitals and Related Institutions, Cincinnati Children's Hospital ranks third among children's hospitals nationwide in number of admissions and first in number of outpatient visits, surgical procedures, and emergency room visits.

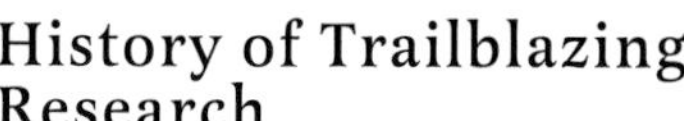

History of Trailblazing Research

In 1931, a contribution from Colonel William Cooper Procter, grandson of the cofounder of Procter & Gamble, helped establish the Children's Hospital Research Foundation. Among the thousands of discoveries and therapeutic programs developed in the past six decades by Cincinnati Children's staff are the first functional heart-lung machine, the first artificial blood compounds used as successful substitutes for whole blood, and a lifesaving medication for respiratory distress syndrome in premature babies.

Today, Cincinnati Children's is expanding programs—funding and hiring world-class scientists in eight research focus areas: fundamental research, molecular medicine, disorders of the neurological system, surgical research, genetics, adolescent medicine, specific diseases of childhood, and health services delivery and prevention.

In 1973, Cincinnati Children's broadened its services through its affiliation with five Cincinnati organizations: the Convalescent Hospital for Children, Adolescent Clinic, Children's Dental Care Foundation, Cincinnati Center for Developmental Disorders (CCDD), and cerebral palsy center. Today, Convalescent Hospital houses the pediatric rehabilitation program, transitional care center, and child psychiatric and behavior units, while Adolescent Clinic, now called Teen Health Center, serves young adults ages 12 to 21. Children's Dental Care Foundation provides general and specialized services for children with complex dental needs. Serving children and adults with developmental disorders such as autism, spina bifida, Downs syndrome, and mental retardation, CCDD helps individuals with developmental disorders to maximize their potential and be contributing members of their community. And United Cerebral Palsy, Inc./Aaron W. Perlman Center for Children provides a wide range of therapeutic programs and services to physically disabled children.

In the 1920s, Cincinnati Children's established an affiliation with the University of Cincinnati that remains strong today. The

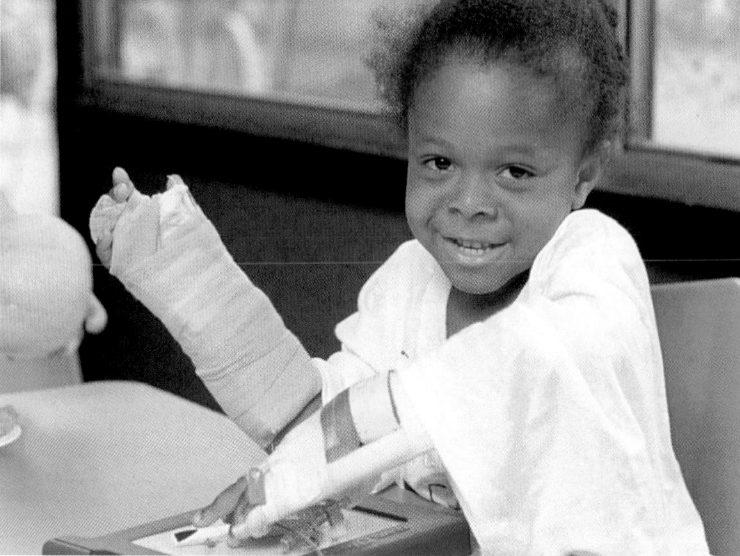

BRUCE CRIPPEN

BRUCE CRIPPEN

When children need specialized medical care—such as liver or stem cell transplants—they come to Cincinnati Children's Hospital Medical Center (top).

Established in 1883, Cincinnati Children's Hospital ranks third among children's hospitals nationwide in number of admissions and first in number of outpatient visits, surgical procedures, and emergency room visits (bottom).

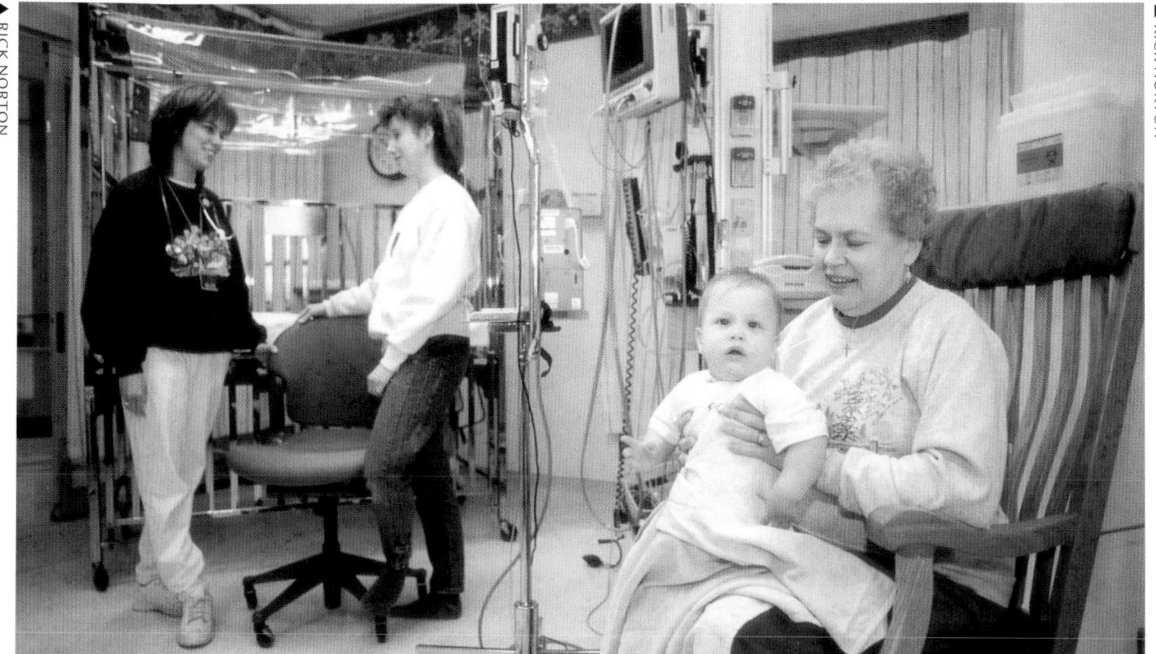

RICK NORTON

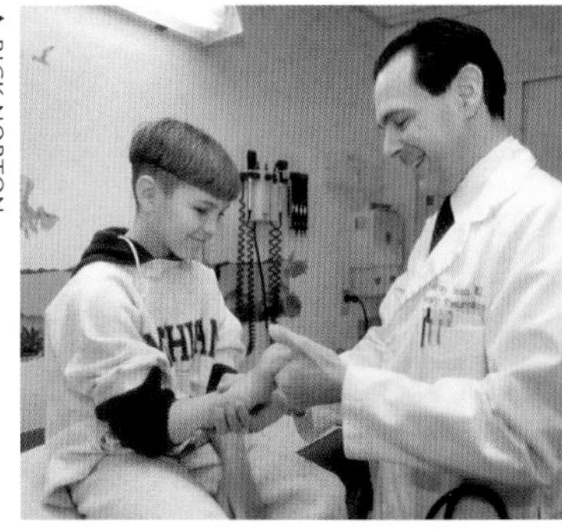

RICK NORTON

Clockwise from top left: Cincinnati Children's brings expert pediatric care close to the children who need it. It partners with many of Greater Cincinnati's hospitals, schools, and community organizations to maintain continuity of care for children in the community.

Among the thousands of discoveries and therapeutic programs developed in the past six decades by the Children's Hospital Research Foundation are the first functional heart-lung machine, the first artificial blood compounds used as successful substitutes for whole blood, and a lifesaving medication for respiratory distress syndrome in premature babies.

As the only pediatric hospital in Greater Cincinnati, Cincinnati Children's is an advocate for children and provides care regardless of a family's ability to pay.

hospital's full-time medical and research staff serve as faculty of the Department of Pediatrics at the university's College of Medicine, underscoring the critical link between teaching, clinical care, and research. Cincinnati Children's has the largest pediatric residency training program within a single U.S. institution, and trains more than 80 percent of the pediatricians, pediatric nurses, and pediatric allied health professionals in Greater Cincinnati.

Reaching Out to the Community

Cincinnati Children's brings expert pediatric care close to the children who need it. It partners with many of Greater Cincinnati's hospitals, schools, and community organizations to maintain continuity of care for children in the community.

Cincinnati Children's outpatient satellite facilities bring pediatric specialty services close to suburban families. At the Hopple Street Neighborhood Health Center, Cincinnati Children's is fulfilling its mission by providing pediatric primary care to a community with great need. With the help of Cincinnati Children's Home Health Care staff, children can return to their homes to continue recovery, or they can stay at home to receive ongoing support for chronic illness.

Cincinnati Children's subspecialists travel many miles to care for children in the region. Pediatric cardiologists, urologists, gastroenterologists, and rehabilitation specialists—among others—regularly visit hospitals in cities, including Portsmouth, Ohio, and Batesville, Indiana. Cincinnati Children's also operates the region's Drug and Poison Information Center, which offers a 24-hour telephone hot line, community outreach, education, and research programs.

In Northern Kentucky, physicians from Cincinnati Children's Emergency Medicine Division staff the emergency department at the St. Elizabeth Medical Center South Unit, in Edgewood, during peak hours. At virtually every hospital with a maternity unit in Greater Cincinnati, Cincinnati Children's neonatologists are on staff to ensure comprehensive care for newborns. More than 20 pediatricians, specializing in the care of infants, work in three teams to staff hospital maternity units.

In addition, Cincinnati Children's helps to improve students' health at Rockdale Paideia Academy. Staffed by Cincinnati Children's, an innovative in-school clinic at Rockdale ensures a child's immediate health needs can be met during each school day.

Dedicated to patient care, research, and education, Cincinnati Children's is currently building a new, state-of-the-art education center. The six-story facility will feature a 300-seat auditorium and a 500-seat dining room, as well as numerous offices, meeting rooms, and classrooms. It will also house the Pratt, CCDD, nursing, and parent and toy libraries. Says Anderson, "This facility will significantly strengthen our ability to meet our important educational mission." Also, Cincinnati Children's has started construction on another addition to the research building and on a new clinical building, which will house inpatient beds, outpatient clinics, and a clinical research facility.

"Our goal is to improve the lives and preserve the health of the entire pediatric community in Greater Cincinnati," Anderson says, "not just the children who come through our many doors."

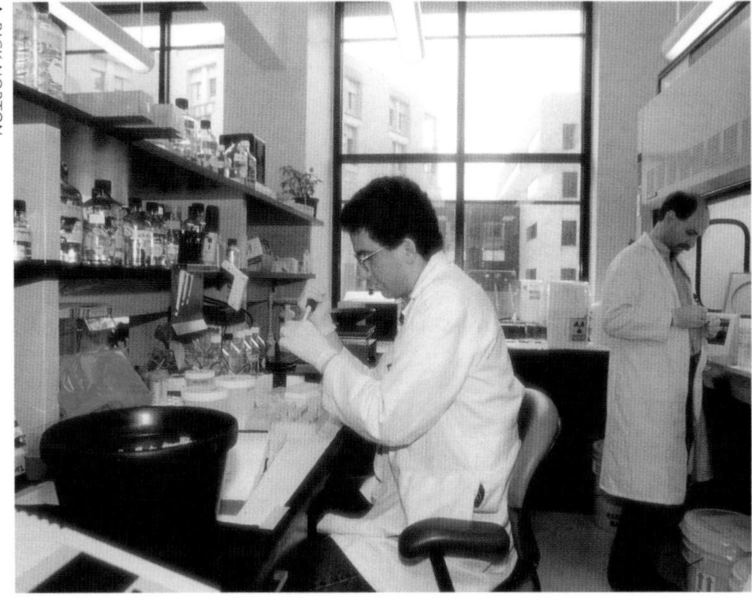

RICK NORTON

The Cincinnati Gear Company

FOR NEARLY A CENTURY, THE CINCINNATI GEAR COMPANY *has been a vital asset to the Greater Cincinnati industrial base. The company began as a component gearing supplier for the booming machine tool industry, and quickly grew into an industry leader. Today, Cincinnati Gear provides gears and gearboxes that help run everything from naval ships to wind turbine generators worldwide.*

In 1907, John Christensen and Soren S. Sorensen laid the foundation for the business that was to become The Cincinnati Gear Company. The two men met while working in Philadelphia at Bilgram Machine Works, a company that manufactured gears and shipped them to the thriving machine tool industry in Cincinnati. With so much business centered in the Cincinnati area, Christensen and Sorensen saw the potential for starting a gear manufacturing company that was closer to its clients. They opened their first factory, the Ohio Bevel Gear Company, on Opera Place in downtown Cincinnati, at a site now occupied by the Skywalk near the corner of Fifth and Race streets.

The company was soon renamed The Cincinnati Gear Company. As the company grew, it moved first to Reading Road and then to the site of its current headquarters in Mariemont, Ohio, east of downtown Cincinnati. In 1974, the company added a second plant at the Mariemont site, and in 1982, Cincinnati Gear opened a plant in Lebanon, New Jersey, to manufacture large gears for a number of industrial and transportation applications, including ships.

Over the next few years, most of the company's operations continued to be centered in the Cincinnati area. To take advantage of the close proximity to the other Cincinnati facilities, Cincinnati Gear relocated the New Jersey plant to Erlanger, Kentucky. Employing more than 75 people, the Erlanger site offered a variety of advantages to The Cincinnati Gear Company's large gear operation. These advantages included a skilled work force, acreage for future expansion, and proximity to the Cincinnati/Northern Kentucky International Airport and to major highways, including Interstates 75 and 275.

Global Expansion

During the 1980s, Cincinnati Gear developed into a high-growth, international business. After the company's acquisition of BHS Sonthofen GmbH in Germany in 1995–now known as the BHS-Cincinnati Getriebetechnik GmbH–The Cincinnati Gear Company became a truly global enterprise. BHS-Cincinnati has a strong presence in industrial markets in Europe and the Pacific Rim, and has significantly expanded Cincinnati Gear's scope to an international level. By combining the companies' capabilities, Cincinnati Gear has become one of the largest

THE CINCINNATI GEAR COMPANY ESTABLISHED ITS PLANT IN ERLANGER BECAUSE OF THE ADVANTAGES NORTHERN KENTUCKY OFFERS: A SKILLED WORK FORCE, ACREAGE FOR FUTURE EXPANSION, AND PROXIMITY TO THE NORTHERN KENTUCKY/GREATER CINCINNATI INTERNATIONAL AIRPORT AND TO MAJOR HIGHWAYS, INCLUDING INTERSTATE 75 AND INTERSTATE 275.

The Cincinnati Gear Company's testing facility can easily accomodate units with more than 50,000 horsepower.

designers and manufacturers of high-power/high-speed gear units in the world. In addition, BHS-Cincinnati continues to specialize in the design and manufacture of high-performance power transmission equipment.

The global development of the company has resulted in 340 employees in The Cincinnati Gear Company operation, 300 in BHS-Cincinnati, and 60 in the Cincinnati Steel Treating Company, for a worldwide total of more than 700 people. Yet, throughout all of its growth and expansion, Cincinnati Gear has remained a locally owned and operated business. The company was under the leadership of the founding Christensen family until 1987, when they sold it to Walter Rye, who had been with the company since 1950 and had been its president since 1978. Currently, he is CEO and chairman of the board, and Frank Posinski is the chief operating officer and president of the company.

"We've expanded our scope considerably over the past few years, but we still maintain a close-knit organization," says Steve Crowell, marketing manager of The Cincinnati Gear Company.

Market Products

Cincinnati Gear's three primary markets are industrial equipment, marine propulsion, and component manufacturing. The industrial equipment market covers many gear applications, including power generation, compressor drives, machine tools, wind power, and over-the-road and off-the-road equipment. The marine market includes gears for a wide range of ships, from large naval vessels to patrol boats, as well as high-speed car and passenger ferries, cargo ships, and mega-yachts. In both lines of business, Cincinnati Gear provides a wide range of standard design and custom-made items sold both domestically and internationally.

"Our competitive edge is our technical expertise and our quality," says Crowell. "We position ourselves as one of the highest-quality gear manufacturers. Cincinnati Gear also has a reputation within the industries it serves for innovative manufacturing techniques." The company has attained an ISO 9001 certification, attesting to the strength of its quality assurance program.

For The Cincinnati Gear Company, one of the keys to the future is the growth and development capabilities of the Erlanger, Kentucky, plant. With room to grow, the plant is a key production facility for the marine and industrial markets, through which its products are sold throughout the world. In addition, Cincinnati Gear will continue to produce the quality products that have made it an important part of the local and national industrial base.

The plant's modern facilities include innovative manufacturing equipment for large gear products.

A NATIONWIDE, CUSTOMER-DRIVEN DISTRIBUTOR OF PRINTING *papers, packaging equipment and supplies, facility supplies and equipment, and graphic imaging prepress equipment and supplies, xpedx is one of the largest companies of its kind in the United States.* ▣ *Headquartered in Covington, Kentucky, the company—which is an affiliate of International Paper—has* nearly 10,000 employees and approximately $7 billion in annual sales. With nearly 120 wholesale distribution centers and 200 stores serving retail customers and small printers, xpedx has 10 million square feet of warehouse space and 1,200 delivery trucks.

Having the advantage of a national network of distribution locations, xpedx focuses on delivering a fully integrated bundle of products at the local level. With technical advisers and sales teams that understand and anticipate customer needs, the company is focused on providing customer solutions while reducing customers' overall cost of operation.

A History of Delivering Service

Excellent service is not new to the company. xpedx was created through the integration of some of the most historic distribution businesses in the country. Names like Dixon Paper in the West, Dillard Paper in the Southeast, Leslie Paper in the Midwest, Carter Rice in the Northeast, and Arvey Paper & Office Products are just some of the companies that have been acquired by xpedx.

During the late 1990s, xpedx grew even larger with the addition of three more companies: Taussig's Graphics Supply, Zellerbach, and Alling & Cory. Through Taussig's, xpedx continues to grow in the area of graphic imaging equipment and supplies distribution. Zellerbach brought to xpedx the expertise and markets of the premier distributor of packaging equipment and supplies in the country. Alling & Cory, the oldest distribution company in the country, added new markets in New York State and other northeastern locations.

While xpedx headquarters moved to Covington in 1992, the Northern Kentucky area was a longtime home for Saalfeld Paper, a distribution company that now is part of the xpedx family. Its originator, Charles Saalfeld, began distributing products from his basement in Covington,

XPEDX DELIVERS EXCELLENCE TO CUSTOMERS IN NORTHERN KENTUCKY, WHERE THE COMPANY'S NATIONAL HEADQUARTERS IS LOCATED IN COVINGTON ON THE OHIO RIVER.

only a few blocks from the current xpedx headquarters. In fact, the location of his business in 1919 was on the same site where the famous MainStrasse clock tower in Covington now stands. As the business grew, it moved across the river, where Cinergy Field now stands. The former Saalfeld Paper now operates out of the Reading Road distribution center in Cincinnati, and is a major distribution location serving customers in Kentucky, Indiana, and Southwest Ohio.

Tom Costello, xpedx president and senior vice president of International Paper, has led the process of bringing together great businesses to build an even greater national distribution company. His vision for his company is based on three fundamentals: customer focus, operational excellence, and people development.

"Focusing on the customer is of significant importance," Costello says. "We need to keep our focus on our customers' needs and how their businesses are changing. Operational excellence is how our own business is run and how we respond to our customers. People development is our third business fundamental. As we continue to understand the nature of our customers, we need to keep building an infrastructure of our own personnel who understand those needs."

xpedx Values and Assets

The company strives to achieve excellence in all aspects of the business. According to Costello, xpedx is succeeding through a commitment to its set of core values and the recognition that its most valued assets are its customers, its employees, and its shareholders. xpedx customers are the focus of the company's commitment to excellence; each employee is dedicated to providing service that contributes to superior value for customers.

In addition, the foundation of the xpedx business is its employees and their personal commitment to excellence. The company recognizes and fosters the development of each individual's potential in a work environment that is safe, challenging, and rewarding. xpedx is equally committed to creating value for its shareholders by achieving superior financial results and growth.

Above all, the company's success is driven by its dedication to customer satisfaction. "We want to be known as our customers' most valued resource," Costello says. "We want to be seen as the most capable, knowledgeable, and dependable supplier for all their graphic arts, paper, packaging, and facility supplies. We want to be their door to the future. We know that if our customers succeed, we will excel."

"We want to be known as our customers' most valued resource," says Tom Costello, president of xpedx.

xpedx works with its customers to provide total solutions to meet all their needs.

Louis Trauth Dairy, Inc.

T'S NO SURPRISE THAT LOUIS TRAUTH DAIRY, INC. HAS PROSPERED *and grown for 80 years. Nor is it surprising that the company has outlasted more than 50 other dairies in Northern Kentucky and Greater Cincinnati. Innovative products and marketing, coupled with a steady expansion and modernization of its production facilities, have made this Newport company what it is today:* the preeminent dairy in the Tri-State region and the only remaining milk and ice-cream plant in Northern Kentucky.

When the Dallas-based Suiza Foods Corporation acquired the company in March 1998, Trauth benefited substantially and also strengthened its position in the business community. Suiza, a progressive and highly aggressive force in the dairy industry nationwide, immediately signaled its intentions by undertaking a multimillion-dollar upgrade of Trauth's processing systems, which doubled the plant's production capacity.

David Trauth, president and CEO of the Newport operations, says Suiza Foods will be looking to shift more production to the Northern Kentucky plant as it consolidates operations. The increased attention and the added investment are creating even more jobs and more opportunities for Trauth in its hometown—something the company and the community have grown accustomed to over the years.

▼ GEORGE SOISTER/GRAPHIC CONCEPTS

UNDER THE LEADERSHIP OF DAVID TRAUTH, PRESIDENT AND CEO, LOUIS TRAUTH DAIRY, INC. HAS BECOME THE PREEMINENT DAIRY IN THE TRI-STATE REGION AND THE ONLY REMAINING MILK AND ICE-CREAM PLANT IN NORTHERN KENTUCKY (TOP).

LOUIS TRAUTH DAIRY HAS CONSISTENTLY BEEN ONE OF THE MOST RECOGNIZED DAIRY BRANDS IN KENTUCKY (BOTTOM).

A Business Based on Innovation

Louis Trauth Dairy proudly showcases its many Kentucky State Fair gold medals in the lobby of its original headquarters on 11th Street in Newport. These awards confirm that the company has consistently been in the forefront of the local dairy industry with an array of consumer-pleasing products. In fact, Trauth was the first dairy in the area to vacuum-pasteurize milk; the first to introduce sweet acidophilus milk; the first to package its sour cream, cottage cheese, and dips in tamper-evident containers; and the first to market 1 Percent Plus a/B milk. In a groundbreaking switch from the industry standard, the company was also the first to replace old-fashioned paperboard milk cartons with convenient, clear-plastic, pint bottles featuring reclosable, screw-on caps—a bold move that immediately sent sales skyrocketing.

In the mid-1980s, the Trauth family began an aggressive growth campaign that included three multimillion-dollar expansions. That process yielded new milk coolers, a temperature-controlled blow-molding facility to manufacture plastic containers, and a supermodern ice-cream plant. The latter includes a computer-automated fast-freeze system, as well as storage and order-picking systems that give Trauth Dairy the ability to consistently deliver fresh ice-cream products in the many varieties consumers demand.

Today, the company produces a dozen types of milk, three varieties of cream, and more than 70 flavors of ice cream, plus eggnog, cottage cheese, assorted dips, and fruit drinks. All of Trauth's quality products are made at its state-of-the-art production and distribution complex in Newport.

A Family Enterprise

The Newport operations began humbly enough in 1920 when Louis J. and Clara Trauth bought a single milk route from Louis's employer, Fred Schuerman's Dairy. Schuerman was considering retirement and wanted to reduce his workload.

The Trauths set up shop behind their home in a 600-square-foot plant at 11th and John streets. Eventually, the whole family was pitching in to run the business, including daughter Helen and sons Louis Jr. and Albert. The business was incorporated in 1956, having been operated as a family partnership up until that point.

The 1968 acquisition of the Niser Ice Cream Co. gave Trauth

an expanded product line that proved to be the catalyst for much of the company's subsequent growth. For example, new freezers in 1972 and 1985 paved the way for a brand-new automated ice-cream plant at 11th and York streets in the early 1990s. Later in the decade, the company also opened a new distribution branch in Louisville and constructed a new building to house its Osgood, Indiana, branch.

Today, numerous family members are still involved in what is now a substantially larger enterprise than Louis J. and Clara Trauth could ever have dreamed. It encompasses four city blocks and 15 acres in the heart of downtown Newport. The founders' grandsons act as the senior management team: Louis Jr.'s son David (president and CEO), along with Albert's sons Steve (vice president of production) and Andy (vice president of engineering).

▲ GEORGE SOISTER/GRAPHIC CONCEPTS

Carl Schultz (left) operates an early wax-milk-carton-packaging machine, while Alex Futscher operates an old manual glass filler (top).

Installed in 1999, Louis Trauth Dairy's 8,000-gallon-per-hour, high-temperature, short-time (HTST) pasteurization unit is the largest in the state of Kentucky (bottom).

Committed to Consumers and Retailers

People across the region who enjoy Trauth Dairy products know that all milk—and, therefore, all ice-cream—is not the same. In fact, Trauth produces milk and ice-cream products with strict quality controls from start to finish. The process begins with the company's careful selection of milk from area dairy farms, which is shipped to the plant in sealed trucks. The milk is immediately tested by Trauth's state-certified laboratory technicians for butterfat, flavor, antibiotics, temperature, and bacteria content. Any raw material that is not up to Trauth's standards is refused.

Once the milk passes the company's rigorous inspection, it is flash pasteurized, homogenized, and then supercooled for packaging. The milk is monitored constantly to guarantee quality and is shipped immediately after being packaged to ensure maximum freshness and shelf life.

Trauth is committed not only to consumers, but also to its retail and institutional customers. These market segments are regarded as critical links in delivering to consumers the freshest, highest-quality dairy products conveniently and at a fair price.

Trauth trains its sales representatives extensively in marketing and merchandising techniques. The company also operates a year-round promotional program, as well as timely seasonal and specialty promotions. In addition, all of

George Soister/Graphic Concepts

George Soister/Graphic Concepts

Clockwise from top:
Louis Trauth Jr., then vice president of the company (left), and Albert Trauth, plant manager, demonstrate the plant's new vacuum pasteurization system, which helped produce a uniform flavor in many gallons of milk.

The Louis Trauth Dairy management team—(seated, from left) Steve Trauth, vice president of production; David Trauth, president and CEO; Andy Trauth, vice president of engineering; (standing from left) Dan Smith, marketing and milk sales manager; Gary Sparks, controller; and Pete Vaughn, ice-cream sales manager—is responsible for the company's innovative products and marketing, and the steady expansion and modernization of its production facilities.

In the filling room at the Newport facility, milk crate conveyors efficiently feed the case packers that ship out more than 270 million pounds of milk a year.

its promotions are backed by an aggressive media advertising effort and by a specialized program that provides products to hospitals, nursing homes, and other institutions.

A Leading Supplier of High-Quality Dairy Products

David Trauth notes that as the dairy industry across the United States is consolidating, so are its major customers. Supermarkets are growing larger, while smaller operators are being bought up as a few national grocery chains gain dominance. This trend mirrors what is happening with convenience stores and institutions such as hospitals, nursing homes, and assisted-living communities.

Given the prevailing conditions in the industry, Suiza Foods is using the opportunity to aggressively acquire regional dairy companies in California, the Southeast, and the Midwest, as well as packaging companies that serve the dairy and other industries.

Suiza has made more than 35 acquisitions since 1988, including 13 dairy companies—one of which was Trauth Dairy—and eight packaging operations in 1998 alone. These acquisitions have more than doubled the company's annual revenue base. Looking to the future, Suiza is continuing its acquisition strategy, pursuing opportunities to expand its markets internationally.

With the commitment of a national company such as Suiza Foods behind it, Louis Trauth Dairy is expected to build on its eight-decade tradition as the leading provider of innovative and high-quality dairy products in Northern Kentucky and Greater Cincinnati.

STOPPING AT THE DIXIE IS A FAMILY TRADITION IN NORTHERN *Kentucky. Just ask the generations of chili lovers who have been eating there for more than 70 years. The kids who come in to get their coneys after the Friday night game know that grandma and grandpa did the same thing when they were kids. College students pile into cars to make road trips in the middle of* the night just to satisfy their coney cravings. And of course, the first and last thing transplanted Northern Kentuckians do when they come back to visit Mom and Pop is get their Dixie three-way fix. True chili aficionados know: The best Cincinnati-style chili in town comes from the oldest chili parlor in Northern Kentucky, Dixie Chili & Deli.

Today, Dixie Chili is a thriving, family-owned and -operated business run by four of Nicholas Sarakatsannis' sons—George, Chris, Panny, and Spiros. There are three company-owned locations in Newport, Erlanger, and Covington, Kentucky, as well as a franchised restaurant in Independence, Kentucky.

The Sarakatsannis family continues to serve premium chili from Papa Nick's secret recipe, using only lean beef chuck or loin, fresh Bermuda onions, fresh garlic, and a secret blending of spices from all over the world. Unlike the reconstituted chili in other parlors, Dixie Chili is made fresh every day by the Sarakatsannis brothers in a USDA-inspected, modern commissary. The Sarakatsannis recipe makes a thick chili with a spicy taste and texture that one reviewer described as "coming together in a great symphonic chord that makes other chili seem confused and random."

WITH SEVERAL LOCATIONS THROUGHOUT NORTHERN KENTUCKY, DIXIE CHILI & DELI IS A THRIVING, FAMILY-OWNED AND -OPERATED BUSINESS RUN BY THE SONS OF FOUNDER NICHOLAS SARAKATSANNIS—(FROM LEFT) GEORGE, CHRIS, PANNY, AND SPIROS.

Dixie Chili is served several different ways. In addition to coneys, there are various combinations offered on the menu, including the exclusive six-way, which is comprised of chili, spaghetti, beans, onions, fresh chopped garlic, and shredded aged cheddar cheese. Dixie Chili can also be used in other recipes, such as chili salad and the famous Dixie Chili Dip.

Years ago, to better accommodate their many customers, the Sarakatsannis family expanded the Dixie Chili menu. These offerings now include lean deli sandwiches, Greek salads with homemade dressing, and a Mediterranean-style vegetarian vegetable soup, as well as other specialty soups, salads, and sandwiches made with natural grain breads from the Big Sky Bread Company.

For avid chili lovers who want to bring a taste of Dixie Chili home, a family pack (a six- or 12-pack of cans) or a Dixie Chili Survival Kit is available at any of the Dixie Chili restaurants or local grocery stores. Those outside of the region can order products by telephone or mail, or through Dixie Chili's Web site at www.dixiechili.com.

Although Papa Nick didn't invent what is now called Cincinnati-style chili, people who know chili believe he perfected it. Dixie Chili & Deli proudly continues to serve his famous recipe to chili lovers throughout Northern Kentucky, and will continue to do so for generations to come.

DIXIE CHILI & DELI PROUDLY CONTINUES TO SERVE ITS FAMOUS RECIPE TO CHILI LOVERS THROUGHOUT NORTHERN KENTUCKY, AND WILL CONTINUE TO DO SO FOR GENERATIONS TO COME (LEFT).

DIXIE CHILI IS SERVED SEVERAL DIFFERENT WAYS. IN ADDITION TO CONEYS, THERE ARE VARIOUS COMBINATIONS OFFERED ON THE MENU, INCLUDING THE EXCLUSIVE SIX-WAY, WHICH IS COMPRISED OF CHILI, SPAGHETTI, BEANS, ONIONS, FRESH CHOPPED GARLIC, AND SHREDDED AGED CHEDDAR CHEESE (RIGHT).

LIKE MANY OF THE HOMES IT'S CONSTRUCTED IN NORTHERN *Kentucky and Cincinnati over the past 70 years, The Drees Company endures, but it isn't outdated. Dramatic growth over the past two decades has made the company the area's largest home builder on either side of the Ohio River. Yet, it remains a family-owned and -oriented business dedicated to building quality homes* that age gracefully, inside and out.

The Drees Company was founded in 1928 by Theodore Drees, a newly arrived German immigrant who bought his initial homesite in Wilder, Kentucky, for $1 down. That first Drees home is still standing, as are more than 17,000 others built since then. Many are owned by obviously satisfied customers who are living in their third or fourth Drees home.

◄ DENNY LANDWEHR

With more than 200 floor plans and literally thousands of customization options, homes built by The Drees Company adhere to quality standards developed through decades of experience.

Enduring Success

At Drees, the company's endurance is considered a direct result of qualities that stand the test of time—convenient locations, gorgeous sites with plenty of green space, timely and intelligent home designs, tireless attention to detail, standardized construction practices, and, perhaps most important, a dedication to creating communities where people want to live.

◄ DENNY LANDWEHR

That kind of dedication starts at the top. In 1958, when Ralph Drees—chairman, chief executive, and son of founder Theodore Drees—developed his very first Drees community, Fairwood Hills in Erlanger, Kentucky, it had one small flaw: the homes were separated from the public school by railroad tracks, and at the time there were no buses to get kids across safely. Drees' response? He bought a Volkswagen van and drove them back and forth for three years.

These days, that tenacious approach to customer service and satisfaction is promoted throughout the organization. The company is composed of multiple profit centers organized according to geography as well as function. Each is empowered to do what it takes to make its customers happy.

A favorite theme at Drees is long-term perspective. The company emphasizes the big picture, but recognizes that execution is accomplished one step at a time. Drees creates successful communities by building fine homes in beautiful settings. It strives for market success by tending to each customer's immediate needs and desires. Organizationally, the firm is structured to give individuals the chance to do their best.

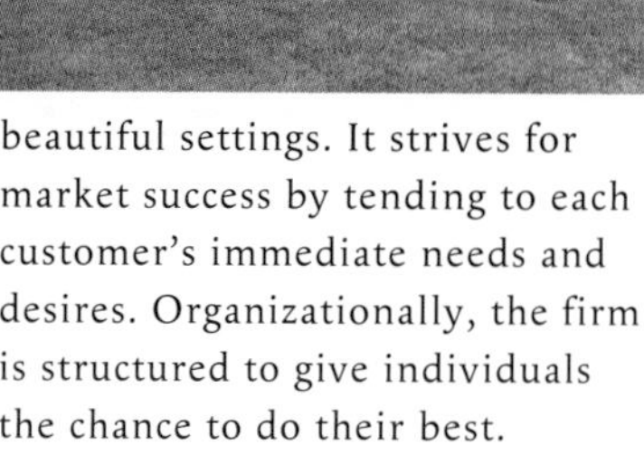

Creating a Community

Creating communities where people want to live means tennis courts, swimming pools, and community centers, but it also translates into an abundance of trees, streams, hills, valleys, nature trails, and picnic areas—natural amenities that let home owners enjoy the great outdoors without leaving their own neighborhoods. Before it breaks ground on a new site, Drees evaluates the land's natural beauty and resources, then adapts its development plans to the site. At Drees' Thornwilde community in Hebron, Kentucky, that kind of approach means including a wildflower preserve and nature trails. Preservation is a primary goal, not an afterthought.

For the homes themselves, there are quality standards developed through decades of experience; an energy-saving program that integrates energy-efficient windows, doors, and insulation with extra-efficient heating and cooling systems; more than 200 floor plans; and literally thousands of customization options. To back up those features, Drees provides 60-day and one-year warranties. And to help buyers get the details exactly the way they want them, there's a Drees design center—another first among area home builders.

Based in Fort Mitchell, Kentucky, Drees now has more than 600 employees and operations in five regional markets across the United States, including Dallas; Austin; Washington, D.C.; Raleigh; and Akron/Canton. Its major focus is on its home market of Northern Kentucky and Southwest Ohio. At last count, the company was active at more than 50 area locations. It builds single-family homes in a broad range of prices for first-time buyers, as well as for people who are moving up. The company introduced town house communities to the market in the 1970s, and now also offers town, carriage, and patio homes to give condominium buyers a variety of options.

Ralph Drees has been the architect of the company's tremendous growth. In order to combat the ups and downs of the economic cycles common in the industry, Drees embraced diversification while remaining dedicated to conservative financial management. Jumping first from Northern Kentucky across the Ohio River to Cincinnati, Drees later moved into other regional markets, adapting the company's strategy to the local conditions.

As a result, Drees operations in the Northern Kentucky/Cincinnati market are highly diversified—ranging from single-family homes, condominiums, apartment complexes, and retail buildings to land development and mortgage financing. Elsewhere—in Dallas, for example—the company limits itself to building upscale homes on land developed by others. The strategy must be working, as Drees has grown from less than $20 million in annual sales in the recession year of 1982 to more than $325 million, on the strength of selling some 1,700 units in 1998. In addition to being the area's largest builder, it's also one of the 50 largest in the United States.

The decade of the 1990s was a time of national recognition for Drees. *Professional Builder* magazine gave the company its National Housing Quality Award in 1994, and honored Ralph Drees as its 1991 National Builder of the Year. The National Association of Home Builders gave him its Legends of Residential Marketing award in 1996, and, in 1998, *Builder* magazine named the company one of America's Best Builders.

Drees has demonstrated long-term success over the last seven decades, and with its dedication to customer satisfaction, attention to detail, and high standards of quality, The Drees Company will be building communities for many more years to come.

The Drees Company was founded by Theodore Drees, a newly arrived German immigrant who completed his first home in Wilder, Kentucky, in 1929.

The family-owned and -oriented business is today run by CEO and Chairman of the Board Ralph A. Drees (right) and COO and President David G. Drees.

Rumpke Consolidated Companies, Inc.

umpke Consolidated Companies, Inc., the local leader in *waste removal, has made a national name for itself by providing state-of-the-art solutions and standout service. Rumpke provides a wide range of garbage removal and recycling-related services, while always keeping the customer first in mind.* ▣ *What began as a small operation founded in the 1930s has grown into an enterprise* that encompasses all facets of waste management. Today, Greater Cincinnati-based Rumpke is the nation's eighth-largest waste management and recycling company based on revenue, with nearly 2,600 employees and 1,600 trucks serving both commercial and residential customers in four midwestern states: Kentucky, Ohio, Illinois, and Indiana.

Tradition of Service

The foundations for Rumpke's steady growth were laid in the 1940s, when brothers Bill and Barney Rumpke moved a small hog farm to 80 acres in northwest Hamilton County's Colerain Township. The farm grew, and the brothers began a profitable waste hauling operation that served many area communities.

Rumpke started out as a family business and has remained a privately owned and family-operated enterprise for its entire 60-plus years. In fact, there are some 80 family members holding various positions throughout the company's 16 subsidiaries. It's no surprise, then, that the company's co-chief executives, Thomas "Tom" Rumpke and William "Bill" Rumpke, are cousins and sons of the founders.

"We've been partners since 1956," says Tom Rumpke on his long-standing relationship with Bill. He credits family involvement as a key to the company's solid reputation. "When Greg or Jeff Rumpke deals with a municipality, there's a comfort level, because our name is on the line. We have all come up through the ranks and know the business inside and out."

Expertise in Gas Processing

The Colerain Township hog farm is now the 440-acre Rumpke Sanitary Landfill, the largest by waste receipts in the state of Ohio. Located 12 miles northwest of downtown Cincinnati, the landfill currently receives an average of 4,200 tons of disposed waste per day, of which approximately 90 percent is hauled by Rumpke. The company also operates nine sanitary landfills, three each in Ohio, Indiana, and Kentucky. Much of Northern Kentucky's disposed waste goes to Rumpke's Pendleton Sanitary Landfill, located six miles north of Falmouth, Kentucky. The landfill, which has served the community since 1972, currently receives an average of 710 tons of disposed waste per day, with a daily limit of 1,500 tons.

All of Rumpke's landfills are classified Subtitle D, which means they meet or exceed all federal and state requirements for modern landfill design and construction. The company maintains its own environmental staff of engineers, geologists, and technicians to oversee the landfill operations.

Aside from being a local landmark and a destination for many school field trips and other interested visitors, the Cincinnati landfill has the distinction of being the site of Ohio's first methane

Rumpke Consolidated Companies, Inc.'s white trucks collect recyclables from bright red bins as part of Rumpke's curbside recycling program. The company collects, processes, and ships more than 300 million pounds of recyclables each year.

gas recovery plant. Rumpke works with GSF, an operating division of Ecogas, to harvest the site's methane gas, which is then purified and sold to the local gas and electric company. The landfill produces enough gas to fill 36 Goodyear blimps every day—the gas currently is used to heat more than 20,000 area homes per day.

At the Forefront of Recycling

Rumpke's services have expanded well beyond its trash removal beginnings: It is now a full-service waste management and recycling company that serves more than 350,000 subscription residential customers and 49,000 commercial customers. In addition to its landfills, Rumpke operates seven transfer stations and 10 recycling centers. Its various operating units offer a host of individualized services as well, including portable rest room rental and hydraulics and engine repair.

Rumpke has always operated with a large measure of foresight in determining future customer waste removal needs and in developing the resources to meet those needs. One example of this is the area of recycling, for which Rumpke has invested heavily in research and development and state-of-the-art technology.

Rumpke's bright red recycling bins are common sights along Cincinnati and Northern Kentucky streets as part of its curbside collection program. The company is a leader in the industry: While some companies are just discovering recycling, Rumpke has been in the forefront of that business for more than 40 years, collecting, processing, and shipping more than 300 million pounds of recyclables annually to end users throughout the Midwest.

Tom Rumpke says the company is the only full-service company offering both recycling and processing of the collected goods. Rumpke Consolidated has managed to automate much of what was a very labor-intensive, manual process of sorting recyclables. Rumpke will continue investing in the area, even in the face of an uncertain market for the goods. "People are more environmentally concerned now," he says. "They care more about how their trash is disposed of."

Giving Back

One of Rumpke's most vital responsibilities is educating the public about the importance of recycling and landfill management. Company employees give recycling and landfill presentations to schools and civic organizations throughout the Midwest. Furthering Rumpke's commitment to the environment, employees participate in many organizations, including the Greater Cincinnati Earth Coalition.

Rumpke also plays a strong role in many of the communities it serves through participation in local chambers of commerce and business clubs, and through charitable giving. After the devastating floods of 1997, the company filled two trucks with cleaning supplies, food, clothing, and toys for the residents of Falmouth, whose 2,700 residents were forced to evacuate when the nearby Licking River disastrously overflowed its banks. Rumpke also received special permission to exceed its limit for disposed waste at its Pendleton County landfill in an effort to help with the massive cleanup efforts.

These efforts, along with a strong commitment to service and innovation, have brought Rumpke Consolidated Companies, Inc. to the forefront of the waste management industry, where—by keeping the customer first in mind—it plans to remain.

Clockwise from top left: Tons of disposed waste delivered daily to the Rumpke Sanitary Landfill in Colerain Township are deposited into cells that have been lined with plastic-composite liner. The visible pipes collect water from the waste and pump it out of the cell for collection.

Rumpke's landfills meet or exceed all federal and state requirements for modern landfill design and construction. Its environmental staff of engineers, geologists, and technicians oversee the laying of impermeable plastic-composite liner.

A Rumpke Front Load Container truck collects waste from one of the many custom-built containers manufactured by Rumpke in different shapes and sizes to fit the customer's needs.

CPO-TV MADE ITS ON-AIR DEBUT JULY 26, 1949, TAKING THE *same call letters as its sister radio station, WCPO-AM. Like the* Cincinnati Post, *the stations were part of Cincinnati-based Scripps Howard. Since television programming was scarce at that stage of the industry's development, WCPO created its own shows to fill the 80 hours or so each week that it broadcast at the time. Soon, it was* one of only two TV stations in the country supplying programming for the networks to rebroadcast. Originally affiliated with ABC, WCPO switched to CBS in 1961, and then returned to ABC in 1996.

Five Decades of Programming

For its first decade, WCPO's programming focus was on entertainment. Its most visible and enduring program was the long-running *Uncle Al Show*, a staple of every area kid's TV diet. The station's regular local news broadcasts began in the summer of 1959. The inaugural news department consisted of news director and anchor Al Schottelkotte, then still a *Cincinnati Enquirer* columnist; news editor Allan White, a *Cincinnati Post* newsman who decided to give television news a one-year trial and ended up staying for the next three decades; and photographer/cameraman Frank Jones. The first newsroom at the station's old Symmes Street studio in Walnut Hills was in the parking lot—a trailer the news team had to share with Uncle Al's equipment.

Allan White recalls that in the news program's infancy, he and Jones would go out during the day and "shoot whatever moved," then call Schottelkotte at the *Enquirer* in the afternoon to piece together 15 minutes of stories for that day's 11 p.m. news. It may not sound like much by today's standards, but the WCPO team was actually developing a concept that would set the nationwide standard for televised news coverage.

Their concept was to take full advantage of television's strength as a visual communications medium and air visuals with every news story. Other stations at the time were solely reliant upon talking heads—anchors sitting behind a desk reading news copy into the camera. Not Al Schottelkotte, who was destined to be the least-shown news anchor in the business, even though he would later win industry and popular acclaim for WCPO's pioneering techniques. Viewers would see Schottelkotte just briefly at the start, at commercial breaks, and at the end—usually less than a minute and a half during a 30-minute newscast. The rest of the time, they would see real-life images of the news, as it happened. One imaginative WCPO innovation was the use of Polaroid instant photos for late-breaking stories. They would

CLOCKWISE FROM TOP:
THE WCPO-TV STUDIO IS LOCATED ON THE CORNER OF 5TH AND CENTRAL IN DOWNTOWN CINCINNATI.

THE STAFF AT WCPO RECOGNIZES AN OBLIGATION TO SERVE A CONGLOMERATION OF HOMETOWNS BOTH NORTH AND SOUTH OF THE RIVER—EACH DISTINCT AND ALL INTERCONNECTED BY THE RIVER AND ITS TRIBUTARIES.

CHANNEL 9 NEWS ANCHORS (FROM LEFT) CLYDE GRAY, RANDY LITTLE, CAROL WILLIAMS, DENNIS JANSON, AND PETE DELKUS ARE FAMILIAR FACES TO VIEWERS THROUGHOUT NORTHERN KENTUCKY.

KAMERAART GROUP

prop up the photo on an easel and show it on TV while the news was being read.

Channel 9 was also the first local station to do a live remote broadcast from a news site, at an event in the 1960s that just happened to take place in Northern Kentucky. Former football-great-turned-political-candidate George Ratterman had been arrested on prostitution-related charges after being set up by organized crime bosses and photographed in a motel room with a stripper known as April Flowers. The trial was held at the Campbell County Courthouse in Newport, and became not only one of the hottest stories of that era, but also one that helped establish local television as a primary source of serious news.

White, who did the Ratterman trial broadcast on the scene, says WCPO used a standard studio camera that had to be taken apart at the studio, transported in pieces in the back of a pickup truck, and then reassembled at the courthouse. When the mob's photographer came clean on the stand and testified that Ratterman had been set up, Ratterman was acquitted, and Channel 9 reported it live from the courthouse. The trial coverage helped establish WCPO's reputation as the source for local news—a reputation that stands today.

Continuing the Tradition

With many other firsts throughout the past five decades, WCPO has built an unmatched news tradition. It has been recognized nationally with numerous citations for news excellence, among them the Alfred I. DuPont, Edward R. Murrow, and Jack R. Howard awards.

Today, WCPO is the flagship station of the Scripps Howard chain and is the only local network-affiliated TV station that is still locally owned. It cherishes and nurtures its reputation as the area's hometown station, even producing a regular feature called *Hometown* with reporter Joe Webb. Other locally produced, homegrown TV shows include *Sports of All Sorts, Know It Alls, Black Memo*, and *Around the House*, as well as regular news features and award-winning investigations by the Channel 9 I-Team.

Always on the leading edge of technology and innovation, WCPO is breaking new ground on the Internet, too. Internet users in the Tri-State area and around the world are just a click away from local news, community information, and more on WCPO's Web site, www.CinciNow.com. In the fall of 1998, the site became the first to provide video streaming of local news stories and major national events. CinciNow.com is evolving to help Channel 9 viewers truly interact with what they see on television. WCPO is working on breakthroughs that will allow its viewers to order products seen on television commercials, get in-depth, detailed news stories, and receive instant coupons on-line.

Then as now, the station regards its market as an entire region that just happens to be dissected by the Ohio River. WCPO recognizes an obligation to serve a conglomeration of hometowns both north and south of the river—each distinct and all interconnected by the river and its tributaries.

Clockwise from top left: Chopper 9, WCPO's state-of-the-art news-gathering helicopter, patrols the skies of Greater Cincinnati for breaking news stories.

Another WCPO first was airborne newsgathering with the 9 Newsbird helicopter.

News director and anchor Al Schottelkotte, one of the pioneers of hard-hitting news at WCPO, was hardly ever seen on *Noon Report*. Viewers would see him just briefly, usually less than a minute and a half during a 30-minute newscast.

One of the longest-running children's shows in the nation and a WCPO institution was *The Uncle Al Show*, hosted by Al Lewis as Uncle Al and Wanda Lewis as Captain Windy.

CHEYENNE'S
AMERICAN
NOVELTIES
625
Spring Stroll

1950-1987

1952 Baptist Life Communities

1954 The St. Luke Hospitals

1955 Maxfield, Schwartz,
Lonnemann & Kohrs, PSC

1958 GBBN Architects

1969 Northern Kentucky
Chamber of Commerce

1970 Drawbridge Estate

1974 Northern Kentucky
Convention & Visitors Bureau

1977 Comair, Inc.

1979 TENTE CASTERS, Inc.

1981 MacKay, Inc.

1982 Spartan Construction

1984 Business Benefits, Inc.

1986 Holland Roofing Group

1987 Tri-County Economic Development
Corporation of Northern Kentucky

Baptist Life Communities

WITH NEW FACILITIES, IMPROVED SERVICES, AND A GROWING *vision, Baptist Life Communities is expanding its Canopy of Care to better meet the needs of Northern Kentucky's senior adults. Founded in 1952 as the Baptist Home, Baptist Life Communities is an outgrowth of the social ministry of the Northern Kentucky Baptist Association, which is made up of more than 60 churches* with more than 30,000 people in the area.

"Our mission has been evolving," explains Director Gary Parker. Originally, the organization provided a specific type of assistance and care for a limited number of senior adults, but as the needs of seniors in the area have changed, so has the mission of Baptist Life Communities. "We are creating a continuum of care, ranging from independent living to subacute and skilled nursing care, all in the same community," Parker says.

This kind of treatment allows seniors to age in place, remaining in the same location as their health care needs change. "We want to take a lot of the worry out of the aging process by providing the services our clients need regardless of their health care or financial situations," Parker explains. Baptist Life Communities calls this concept its Canopy of Care.

With new facilities, improved services, and a growing vision, Baptist Life Communities is expanding its Canopy of Care to better meet the needs of Northern Kentucky's senior adults.

Twin Philosophies

Baptist Life Communities operates with two distinct but interwoven philosophies known as Quality and Caring. The organization takes pride in providing the very best in professional services. The nursing facilities, which are accredited by the Joint Commission on Accreditation of Healthcare Organizations, maintain excellence in state and federal quality standards.

Baptist Life Communities promotes an atmosphere of caring concern throughout its staff and residents. "We believe that human caring is as important to health and well-being as quality technical services," Parker asserts, "and it is very reassuring to live in a community where both management and neighbors are looking out for your best interest."

Special Settings for Special People

The first facility sponsored by Baptist Life Communities, the Baptist Home proudly boasts one of the most magnificent settings in the Tri-State region. Perched atop a hill in South Newport, the Baptist Home provides a scenic, panoramic view of the Cincinnati skyline and the surrounding communities.

Equally stunning is the organization's second facility, the Baptist Village, which was established in Erlanger, Kentucky, in 1995. Located on 21 rolling hills, the Baptist Village offers stylish Georgian colonial designs and comfortable elegance for senior adult living.

Baptist Life Communities is developing a third facility, called Baptist Towers, at 800 Highland Avenue in Covington. The attractively remodeled facility will offer secure and tasteful living for 112 senior adults.

Plans are also under way for a fourth Baptist Life community on a 46-acre farm in Burlington. This pastoral setting will become a home for 178 senior adult families. With spacious greens and colonial- and Victorian-styled structures, Griesser Farm is designed to be unrivaled in its beauty and serenity.

Baptist Life Communities' approach to health care is not about houses and land; it is about people. "We believe God has called us to serve people," Parker concludes. "As the needs of our clients have grown and changed, so have the mission and ministry of Baptist Life Communities. We will continue growing to meet those needs in the next millennium."

Baptist Life Communities' Canopy of Care allows seniors to age in place, remaining in the same location as their health care needs change.

HAT CAN'T BE SEEN IN A BUILDING IS OFTEN MORE IMPORTANT *than what can be seen. For more than 40 years, the engineering firm of Maxfield, Schwartz, Lonnemann & Kohrs, PSC (MSLK) has been designing all of the elements for the infrastructure of buildings, successfully having a hand in creating thousands of safe, sturdy, and comfortable facilities.* *The company began in Covington in* 1955 and has been housed at the same historic brick building at Fifth and Madison streets since 1958. Specializing in electrical and mechanical engineering services, MSLK has grown to include new engineering disciplines, and employs more than 20 highly trained and educated engineers, draftsmen, and support people. The company's list of accomplishments now includes more than 3,800 projects nationwide.

Most of the firm's projects, however, have been on sites in and around Cincinnati and Northern Kentucky. MSLK's vast body of local work has been for both high-profile projects used by the public, as well as lower-profile projects for private clients. At the fast-growing Cincinnati/Northern Kentucky International Airport in Boone County, MSLK has played a key role in the numerous phases of expansion, including the design of the widespread facility's high-voltage electrical distribution system, which delivers power through more than 200 miles of conduit and wire. St. Elizabeth Medical Center, Thomas More College, and the new Newport Aquarium have also benefited from the firm's engineering know-how.

New Area of Emphasis

As a full-service firm, MSLK provides most of what remains unseen in a building but is essential to its ultimate performance—mechanical, electrical, plumbing, fire protection, and communication technology engineering are all critical components of safe and livable buildings.

The firm's recently added communication technology services bring its clients the latest in specialized wiring for data, network, telephone, and security systems. "In order to meet client expectations, we felt it was necessary to expand the communication side of the business," explains MSLK President Joe Kohrs. "Audiovisual room integration is one of the services we're providing at this point. In the future, this technology, due to its complexity, will be one of the driving forces in our industry."

All of the firm's services must be performed with a focus on the needs of those ultimately using the structure, and must be cost effective and energy efficient as well. The design of plumbing, heating, air-conditioning, ventilation, power distribution, lighting, fire protection, communication, and security systems all have specialized requirements dictated by the industry served.

MSLK has performed work in numerous fields, for facilities such as hospitals, colleges, office buildings, manufacturing sites, and churches. The firm counts as one of its strengths the diversity of projects for which it has been hired as an engineering consultant. "Our goal is continuous improvement in all fields," Kohrs says.

The company's commitment to quality, its attention to innovative services and technologies, and its long history of satisfying the needs of clients around the country ensure the continued success of Maxfield, Schwartz, Lonnemann & Kohrs well into the next millennium.

▶ Robin Victor Goetz

Maxfield, Schwartz, Lonnemann & Kohrs partners (from left) Bob Heil, Joe Kohrs, and Rob Lonnemann survey plans for the Newport Aquarium. The firm's involvement in the aquarium project included the design of plumbing, HVAC, electrical service, and electrical distribution.

The St. Luke Hospitals

FROM BROKEN BONES TO BRILLIANT DOCTORS TO BIRTHING *babies, Northern Kentuckians trust The St. Luke Hospitals with their health care needs. St. Luke proudly serves these growing needs through its many facilities, including St. Luke Hospital East in Fort Thomas, St. Luke Hospital West in Florence, the St. Luke Alcohol and Drug Treatment Center in Falmouth, and the Louise* Southgate Family and Women's Center in Bellevue.

With nearly 1,800 employees, more than 500 affiliated physicians, and hundreds of dedicated volunteers and auxilians, The St. Luke Hospitals have built a tradition of being the first to offer the newest and best health care technology and services.

IN THE 1990S, ST. LUKE WEST IN FLORENCE HAS ADDED THE 70,000-SQUARE-FOOT EMERGENCY/OUTPATIENT BUILDING, A 16-BED BIRTHING CENTER, AND THE CHILDREN'S PAVILION, WHICH PROVIDES STATE-OF-THE-ART MEDICAL ATTENTION THROUGH THE PEDIATRIC URGENT CARE CENTER.

A Half Century of Growth

The tradition of excellence began when St. Luke opened in 1954. Six years earlier, Campbell County voters had passed a bond issue to establish the hospital in Fort Thomas. The hospital began expanding immediately, and by 1963, had opened two new floors. An intensive care unit and Northern Kentucky's first coronary care unit were added in the early 1970s.

The 1980s proved to be a time of phenomenal growth for The St. Luke Hospitals. The Fort Thomas hospital built a patient bed tower and parking garage. In 1980, St. Luke purchased the Pendleton County Hospital in Falmouth, which now serves as the inpatient St. Luke Alcohol and Drug Treatment Center.

The greatest expansion took place in 1989 when St. Luke acquired the William E. Booth Memorial Hospital in Florence. Now known as St. Luke Hospital West, it has undergone many expansions to meet the needs of the rapidly growing Boone County area. In the 1990s alone, St. Luke West has added the 70,000-square-foot Emergency/Outpatient Building, a 16-bed birthing center, and the Children's Pavilion, which provides state-of-the-art medical attention through the Pediatric Urgent Care Center.

Children's services are integral to The St. Luke Hospitals. St. Luke has two Children's Advocacy Centers for the detection and treatment of child abuse, as well as two St. Luke Pediatric Centers. Since 1987, the Children's Advocacy Center (CAC) has served as a strong resource for children in need. The only child abuse center in Northern Kentucky, CAC has assisted more than 2,000 children and their family members.

ESTABLISHED IN FORT THOMAS IN 1954, ST. LUKE HOSPITAL EAST HAS BEEN EXPANDING CONSTANTLY. NOW WITH 310 BEDS, THE HOSPITAL RECENTLY EXPANDED ITS CARDIOLOGY AND RADIOLOGY SERVICES.

Times Are Changing

In 1995, St. Luke joined the Health Alliance, a consortium of area hospitals that strive to provide an integrated, cost-effective regional health care delivery system. Other members of the Health Alliance are The Christ Hospital, The University Hospital, The Jewish Hospital, and The Fort Hamilton Hospital, as well as the physicians of Alliance Primary Care.

St. Luke is also part of the Commonwealth Health Alliance, a partnership of 40 Kentucky hospitals. These affiliations ensure that St. Luke patients receive the best health care at any member facility.

Committed to Community Health

The St. Luke Hospitals are committed to the community in a number of ways. One of our key objectives focuses on community health," says Daniel M. Vinson, senior vice president of operations. "We offer a proactive approach to the good health of Northern Kentuckians by providing them with up-to-date information, state-of-the-art technology, and a highly trained, caring staff. Charitable commitment is also key at St. Luke. We help support a variety of non-profit organizations and maintain strong community ties."

St. Luke showed its commitment to the fight against cancer in 1981, when it opened the Northern Kentucky Cancer Treatment Center, the first facility of its kind in the area. A second Cancer Treatment Center opened in 1998 at St. Luke West. Together, the centers take a

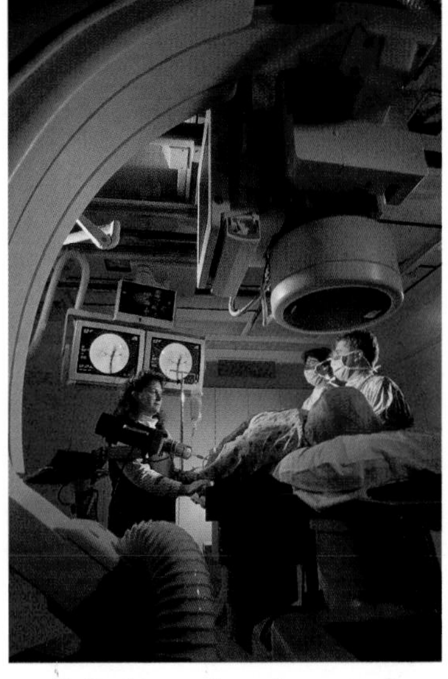

Top left: Cardiac services are at the heart of many expansions at St. Luke. The St. Luke Hospitals' two Cardiology Centers offer echo-cardiograms, stress echo, Holter monitoring, and cardiac event monitoring.

Top right: St. Luke is a leader in providing the latest state-of-the-art technology for patient care patient care, including new digital imaging equipment for the Radiology Department.

holistic approach to cancer treatment that includes nutritional, emotional, and spiritual support for patients and their families, as well as comprehensive oncology services. Accredited by the American College of Surgeons, the centers are a research site for the National Cancer Institute.

Another of The St. Luke Hospitals' many firsts in Northern Kentucky is its Birthing Center. St. Luke introduced LDRP (labor-delivery-recovery-postpartum) birthing suites in 1986, and the LDRPs are now the choice for nearly 2,000 mothers each year. The Birthing Center also offers adoptive parenting preparation classes, mother-to-be exercise programs, and Northern Kentucky's first full-time breast-feeding educator.

As with birthing and cancer treatment services, St. Luke has led the way in cardiac care. It opened Northern Kentucky's first Phase II Cardiac Rehabilitation and Wellness Center in 1986. These facilities are geared to meet the needs of patients who have undergone heart procedures or who have diabetes or lung problems.

Cardiac Rehab recently expanded its services at the original St. Luke East location and opened a second center at St. Luke West in 1999.

Cardiac services are at the heart of many expansions at St. Luke. The Cardiology Centers of The St. Luke Hospitals now offer the most modern, efficient catheterization equipment in the Tri-State area. The new system is a filmless digital system that is expected to become the worldwide standard. Filmless digital systems enable the cardiologist to view the procedure in real time, thereby expediting diagnosis and treatment. Both Cardiology Centers offer echo-cardiograms, stress echo, Holter monitoring, and cardiac event monitoring.

Meeting Special Needs

St. Luke has been a leader in the development of specialty programs that deliver a wide range of diverse, convenient services. Its hospitals house an OccNet center, sleep disorders centers, a Mental Health Partial Hospitalization pro-gram, diabetes centers, and a comprehensive physician referral service.

"The future looks bright for The St. Luke Hospitals," Vinson says. "St. Luke is committed to the community and will continue to flourish with it. We hope generations of Northern Kentuckians will continue to trust The St. Luke Hospitals."

St. Luke introduced the Birthing Center in 1986, and it is now the choice for nearly 2,000 mothers each year. It also offers adoptive parenting preparation classes, mother-to-be exercise programs, and Northern Kentucky's first full-time breast-feeding educator (bottom left).

The St. Luke Hospitals opened Northern Kentucky's first Phase II Cardiac Rehabilitation and Wellness Center in 1986. These facilities are geared to meet the needs of patients who have undergone heart procedures or who have diabetes or lung problems (bottom right).

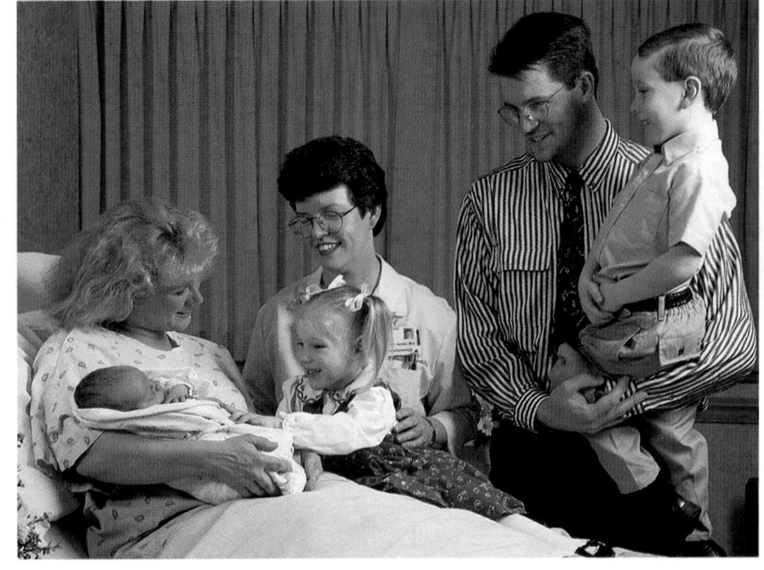

OUNDED IN 1958, GBBN ARCHITECTS HAS GROWN TO ELEVEN *partners, 33 registered architects, and 80 total employees with offices in downtown Cincinnati and Lexington, Kentucky. The firm provides services in architecture, interiors, planning, and engineering for all sizes and categories of buildings and building complexes. GBBN has managed architectural design, renovation, and planning services on* more than 2,500 projects and has received numerous awards for design excellence.

Clockwise from top: GBBN Architects is guided by its partners: (seated, from left) John B. Gartner Jr., AIA; Christopher N. Beghtel, AIA; Robert E. Gramann, FAIA; Joseph T. Schwab, AIA; (standing, from left) Keven M. Speece, AIA; Alan J. Warner, AIA; Kimberly D. Patton, AIA; John W. Rogers, AIA; and Gregory A. Otis, AIA. Not pictured are Matthew J. Birk and Ken Greene, AIA.

The Newport Aquarium, a GBBN project, is a 60,000-square-foot facility at the Newport on the Levee center, and has become the catalyst for commercial and entertainment redevelopment in the city. It features fresh and saltwater habitats, as well as several walk-through tanks.

Designed by Cesar Pelli & Associates, the Aronoff Center for the Arts in Cincinnati demonstrates GBBN's ability to manage large design teams with a construction manager to deliver a complete project on time and within budget.

High Standards of Quality

GBBN boasts a proven track record with respect to high-profile, urban, public-funded projects. Accounts such as the Aronoff Center for the Arts, the Hamilton County William Howard Taft Center, the Alms & Doepke Building, and the expansion of the main branch of the Public Library of Cincinnati and Hamilton County demonstrate GBBN's ability to excel in a field where cost and schedule are critical, and to maintain high standards of quality and "constructability."

GBBN Architects is accustomed to working with and orchestrating large project design teams that, on highly visible public projects, have included signature design architects who have project-specific expertise. The practice is built on repeat business from satisfied clients encompassing a variety of projects in both size and complexity.

GBBN makes sure its principal architects are actively involved in each project; this attention assures clients that they will receive the responsiveness and the efficiency they deserve.

The firm has the ability to manage large design teams (more than 13 consultants) with a construction manager to deliver a complete project on time and within budget. For example, the 215,000-square-foot Aronoff Center for the Arts, designed by Cesar Pelli & Associates and built by GBBN, contains a 2,700-seat Broadway House theater, a 440-seat intermediate theater, a 150-seat black box theater, and several support offices.

Another of GBBN's projects, the Newport Aquarium is a new, 60,000-square-foot facility on the Ohio River, and has become the catalyst for commercial and entertainment redevelopment in the city. The concepts of the 15 exhibit areas range from fresh and saltwater habitats of the tiniest and most docile sea creatures to a walk-through tank containing several species of sharks. The exhibition area also includes a theater, restaurant, gift shop, and traveling exhibit hall.

N THE LATE 1960S, JERRY DETERS, AN ALREADY SUCCESSFUL *Northern Kentucky home builder, decided to diversify his business. While attending a meeting in Texas, he heard about a fellow builder who had finished construction on a hotel. Deters thought about it over a cup of coffee, and decided to build a very special hotel of his own. ▣ He started with a motel, which opened in 1970. The inn* at Interstate 75 and Buttermilk Pike shared the landscape with several service stations. Some thought the location—five miles south of Cincinnati—was a poor choice. The conventional wisdom was that hotels belonged in the city.

More than a quarter century after that decision, Deters proved that conventional wisdom was wrong: The big growth area in the hospitality industry has been in Northern Kentucky, much of it centered at Deters' Drawbridge Estate.

Known for the consistent application of Tudor themes in its architecture and decoration, the Drawbridge Estate provides unique surroundings for its guests. The site of many corporate group meetings, conventions, association gatherings, and private parties, the inn recently completed a $3 million renovation of its interior.

Something for Everyone

Today, the Drawbridge Estate complex covers 23 acres and offers an array of amenities, including the Drawbridge Inn, three restaurants, four lounges, 18 meeting rooms, and three swimming pools. Adding to the estate's attraction is the Oldenberg Brewery & Entertainment Complex, immediately adjacent to the inn.

The Drawbridge Inn, the second-largest hotel in the Greater Cincinnati area, offers 505 guest rooms and attracts 160,000 overnight guests annually. In the 28-year history of Deter's hostelry, more than 3 million guests have stayed at the inn.

Known for the consistent application of Tudor themes in its architecture and decoration, the Drawbridge Estate provides unique surroundings for its guests. It is the site of corporate group meetings, conventions, association gatherings, and numerous private parties. The estate's London Hall seats 1,500 people in a theater-style configuration.

Other attractions, located inside the Drawbridge proper, include Josh's, serving Continental cuisine in an English hunt club setting, and Chaucer's 24-hour restaurant. A short walk away, The Gatehouse Taverne exudes medieval charm. The restaurant features prime meats and fine wines, and the salad bar would satisfy Henry the VIII.

Drawbridge caters to business and leisure travelers. "We treat you like this is your home away from home," says James Willman, vice president of operations. "Our rooms have a homey feel, with residential-type furniture and patterned wallpaper. Our employees are trained to make travelers feel like they're a guest in someone's home."

The growth of the aviation industry in the area has also been an important stimulus to the Drawbridge. Deters has served on the board of directors of the Cincinnati/Northern Kentucky International Airport, and the inn is the designated crew base for Delta Air Lines. Both the airport and downtown Cincinnati are less than a 10-minute drive from the Drawbridge, the center of social activity for Northern Kentucky.

To continue to please its guests, the inn recently completed a $3 million renovation of its interior. In addition, it offers special programs that are growing in popularity. Among them are weekend getaway packages, and one of the Drawbridge's most popular offerings, a romantic weekend escape, which combines secluded accommodations, champagne, chocolates, and a gift certificate toward dinner.

For nearly 30 years, Drawbridge Estate has been entertaining travelers and making guests feel at home. Today, the conventional wisdom is that Drawbridge Estate will continue to be an important part of a fast-growing region for many years to come.

A cluster of restaurants is located at the Drawbridge Estate, including Josh's Restaurant (left), which serves Continental cuisine in an English hunt club setting; Chaucer's 24-hour restaurant; and the medieval-flavored Gatehouse Taverne (right), which features prime meats and fine wines.

Northern Kentucky Chamber of Commerce

The Northern Kentucky Chamber of Commerce represents *nearly 2,000 businesses and their more than 100,000 employees in 39 cities and three counties—Boone, Campbell, and Kenton—as well as members outside the area. Approximately 75 percent of its member businesses employ 25 people or fewer locally. Each year, more than 8,000 business leaders attend various Chamber-*sponsored events, and in excess of 1,200 volunteers give their time and effort to numerous Chamber-sponsored programs.

These numbers speak to the scope of the Northern Kentucky Chamber of Commerce. The organization represents a large and diverse region with a true entrepreneurial spirit, and it nurtures small start-up businesses, as well as large national and multinational corporations. More important than numbers and percentages, however, are the Northern Kentucky Chamber of Commerce's long history and its promising future of cooperation, determination, resourcefulness, and accomplishment.

A History of Success

The Northern Kentucky Chamber of Commerce was formed in 1969, when members of the Campbell County and Kenton-Boone chambers of commerce voted overwhelmingly to merge. At that time, Ed Hengelbrok Jr., president of the Campbell County Chamber of Commerce, and H. Gordon Martin, president of the Kenton-Boone Chamber of Commerce, believed that by combining their efforts and merging the two chambers into one entity, they could better promote area businesses and help facilitate decisions affecting not just one or two counties, but the entire region.

The Northern Kentucky Chamber of Commerce was established on Scott Street in Covington, with Walter L. Pieschel, a sales manager at the Northern Kentucky Coca-Cola Bottling Plant, as its first president. The first priorities of the fledgling chamber were the completion of Interstate 275 through the region and the expansion of Northern Kentucky University from a two-year community college into a four-year independent institution.

Since its founding, the Northern Kentucky Chamber of Commerce has played an extremely active role in the region's business and economic arena. The organization has been instrumental in founding Big Bone State Park in Union, Kentucky; forming the Northern Kentucky Area Development District in 1971; raising money for the Transit Authority of Northern Kentucky; creating the Leadership Northern Kentucky program in 1978; and forming the Tri-County Economic Development Corporation in 1986. The Chamber has also been very active in the development of the regional airport. It helped raise several million dollars for an expansion in 1990, and lobbied to have the name changed from the

Clockwise from top:
The Northern Kentucky Chamber of Commerce was established at 225 Scott Street in Covington, with Walter L. Pieschel, a sales manager at the Northern Kentucky Coca-Cola Bottling Plant, as its first president.

In 1999, the Chamber moved to new offices at the Chamber Center in Fort Mitchell, a highly accessible area for serving its membership.

Forty-five organizations receive orientation as charter members of the Chamber's Workforce Development Collaborative (WDC). The WDC is providing the catalyst for workforce readiness and educational reform in the area.

Greater Cincinnati International Airport to the Cincinnati/Northern Kentucky International Airport.

Present and Future

With a history rich with accomplishment and success, the Northern Kentucky Chamber of Commerce is working toward the future. Now located in new offices in the Chamber Center in Fort Mitchell, the Chamber is strategically poised and looking forward to the new millennium.

In 1991, the Chamber formed the Capital Consensus Committee under the leadership of John Finnan, with the intention of focusing and intensifying Northern Kentucky's voice in the state legislature. Now headed by Gary Bricking, the committee identifies the region's capital and transportation needs, and works with national, state, and local governments to see that those needs are met. Examples of the committee's tremendous success include the funding secured for the Northern Kentucky Convention Center and the Science Center at Northern Kentucky University.

The Quest Report has yielded similarly impressive results. In 1996, hundreds of local volunteers worked to identify Northern Kentucky's potential—specifically, what the area could achieve by 2020. The findings were published in the *Quest Report: A Vision for Northern Kentucky*. In response to the report, Forward Quest was created to implement the report's goals. Out of the Quest visioning process have come the new River Walk, the Metropolitan Growth Alliance, SouthBank Partners, and the Millennium Monument in Newport.

In 1998, the Chamber started an innovative partnership with business, education, and the community to tackle the problem of workforce readiness. The Workforce Development Collaborative was formed to address the workforce shortage and workforce quality issues.

The Benefits of Membership

The Northern Kentucky Chamber of Commerce offers its members four key benefits. The first of these involves business promotion and interaction: The Chamber actively supports its members through an annual membership directory that is circulated to more than 7,000 customers, and all members are listed on the Chamber's Web site, www.nkycc.org. Members have numerous opportunities to promote their businesses through advertising and sponsorship of Chamber events and programs. The Chamber is volunteer driven, and members make invaluable business contacts through a wide variety of Chamber activities throughout the year.

Another benefit of Chamber membership is business advocacy. In addition to employing a full-time staff lobbyist and working with the Capital Consensus Committee, the Chamber manages the Business Government Affairs Council, which is charged with tasks that include maintaining Northern Kentucky's presence on a state level in Frankfort and on a national level in Washington, D.C. These efforts keep Chamber members abreast of business and legal issues that may affect their businesses.

In addition, the Chamber also offers its members a variety of cost-saving benefits, including health care, cellular phone, and long-distance service.

The fourth benefit, and the end product of all services the Chamber offers, is community enrichment. This is perhaps the most important, as it affects not only the business region, but also the quality of life for all Northern Kentuckians as well.

The Chamber operates under the realization that change does not happen by chance. By working closely with area businesses, organizations, and government agencies, the Chamber is making Northern Kentucky's present better than its past and its future better than its present.

Clockwise from top left:
Eggs 'N Issues, a monthly breakfast meeting featuring topics and speakers addressing Northern Kentucky issues, is the longest-running Chamber program—29 years—and is attended monthly by some 200 members and guests.

Member companies of all sizes benefit from participating in bimonthly Leads Group meetings. Hundreds of business referrals are shared by members at these interactive meetings.

Northern Kentucky is represented by members of the Chamber's U.S. Legislative Task Force annually in Washington when they present before regional members of Congress a priority agenda based on the needs of member firms and the community.

Northern Kentucky Convention & Visitors Bureau

SINCE ITS ESTABLISHMENT IN 1974, THE NORTHERN KENTUCKY *Convention & Visitors Bureau has been charged with bringing visitors and conventions into the region it represents. In filling that role, this vital organization has been responsible for much of the area's steady growth and has made tremendous strides in affecting the area's economic impact. Over the past decade, for example,* Northern Kentucky has experienced unsurpassed expansion in nearly every market segment.

"By and large, a convention and visitors bureau is the first stepping stone one has into a community," says Sheree Allgood, manager of communications for the Northern Kentucky Convention & Visitors Bureau. "Northern Kentucky is unique in its tremendous growth. Its attractiveness for leisure travelers and for corporate clientele really can't be beat. We are reasonable in price and easy to get to, and we offer so much to our visitors."

One of Northern Kentucky's newest attractions is the Oceanic Adventures Newport Aquarium, a privately financed venture on Newport's historic riverfront (bottom right).

The John A. Roebling Suspension Bridge (bottom left), built just after the Civil War, and the 100-foot-tall Carroll Chimes Tower (top), which houses 43 bells and boasts carvings depicting the story of the Pied Piper of Hamelin, date back to Northern Kentucky's history as a river port.

Wide-Ranging Amenities and Attractions

Many of the area's top attractions date back to Northern Kentucky's history as a river port. The John A. Roebling Suspension Bridge, for example, is among the first of its kind, but was met with initial skepticism when it was built just after the Civil War. Today, the bridge still provides a vital link between Cincinnati and Covington, and is both a regional landmark and a tourism booster. There is also the 100-foot-tall Carroll Chimes Tower, located in the heart of historic MainStrasse Village in Covington. Housing 43 bells in a German Gothic tower, the structure boasts carvings that depict the story of the Pied Piper of Hamelin.

First and foremost among Northern Kentucky's wide range of amenities is the Cincinnati/Northern Kentucky International Airport, which serves as a catalyst for growth by making the region accessible for all types of travelers. Open for business since 1947, the airport is today one of the fastest growing in the country. By the year 2010, it is expected to become one of the 10-largest airports in the world.

More recently completed attractions include Oceanic Adventures Newport Aquarium, a privately financed venture on Newport's historic riverfront. Linking Covington with Cincinnati, Newport, and Bellevue is the newly developed Southbank Shuttle, a low-cost bus service that provides mass transportation for visitors on both sides of the Ohio River. The newest jewel in Northern Kentucky's crown is the recently completed convention center in Covington.

Accommodations and Restaurants

One of the major goals of the Northern Kentucky Convention & Visitors Bureau is to promote the region's many hotels, motels, and bed-and-breakfasts. Says Allgood, "Once visitors are here, we can show them the attractions, museums, the nightlife, our historic towns, and everything else that people who live here have grown to love."

Among the many things that both visitors and residents seem to love are Northern Kentucky's diverse dining options. Whether they serve five-star, French meals or bowls of famous Cincinnati-style chili, restaurants on the river in Kenton and Campbell counties have been a major draw, and their continued success bodes well for the region's economic health.

According to Allgood, the ultimate prosperity of Northern Kentucky and its numerous assets depends on regional cooperation among the many levels of business and government. "One of the critical factors for our success here is that everybody in Northern Kentucky is involved on a regional scale," she concludes. "Without that kind of cooperation, we wouldn't be able to enjoy the successes we have had in recent years."

Both literally and figuratively, Comair, Inc. continues to *soar ahead in the flight industry as its operations rise to new heights. The Northern Kentucky-based airline has been so successful at redefining industry standards that many people no longer regard it as merely a regional airline. Rather, they appreciate what sets Comair apart from the average airline, and passenger* boardings and the miles they log continue to increase substantially each year.

Passengers appreciate Comair's first-rate service, which includes setting up, in conjunction with partner Delta Air Lines, the first hub in North America to provide jet service to each of the hub's destinations. And the service promises to get even better, thanks to the addition of dozens of new Canadair Regional Jets. The quietest such jets in the world, all are powered by General Electric engines and manufactured by Bombardier Aerospace of Canada. The 50- to 70-seat aircraft can cruise at upwards of 500 miles per hour and offer passengers a two-by-two seating configuration, with no middle seats to impede the comfort of Comair travelers.

"Comair pioneered the use of regional jets, and it remains the leading operator of regional jets in the world," says David A. Siebenburgen, president and chief executive officer of the airline. "Our goal is to be an all-jet carrier by 2001—the first regional carrier in the U.S. with an all-jet fleet."

Comair introduced regional jet aircraft to the U.S. flying public in 1993, and was met immediately with skepticism from industry analysts and rivals who felt that the expensive jets were not financially feasible. Comair proved otherwise, leaving other regional carriers behind while providing its own passengers with comfort and convenience. More seats, longer ranges, faster flight times, and lower costs have enabled Comair to offer more frequent flights, as well as service to destinations that are outside the range of non-jet aircraft. Since switching to jets, the number of passengers the company enplanes annually has more than doubled. Comair now serves 85 cities, from Montreal to Nassau to Colorado Springs.

▸ BOMBARDIER AEROSPACE OF CANADA

Clockwise from top:

With more than 700 flights daily, Comair, Inc. flies to 85 cities, from Montreal to Nassau to Colorado Springs, serving more than 6 million customers annually.

Ever Upward

Since it was founded in 1977 by the father-son team of Raymond and current Comair Chairman David Mueller, the company has succeeded and grown at every turn. Its Delta Connection partnership with Delta Air Lines was established in 1984 and solidified in 1986 with the Comair/Delta hub at Cincinnati/Northern Kentucky International Airport. In 1987, the airlines announced the joint development of a hub in Orlando.

In 1994, Comair dedicated a new, 53-gate terminal concourse at the Boone County airport, giving it the world's largest regional airline facility. In 1998, Comair announced a $40 million expansion of its airport headquarters, maintenance and training facilities, concourse, and corporate hangar.

With the completion of these projects, Comair will employ about 5,000 people in Northern Kentucky. Area residents also benefit from Comair's innovative marketing programs, including a code-sharing agreement with Belgium's Sabena Airlines and a low-cost, weekend travel program that makes flying to any Comair destination very affordable. For Comair and its passengers, the sky's the limit as the company continues to uphold a tradition of efficient service and standard-setting quality.

▸ JIM CALLAWAY

In 1994, Comair dedicated a new, 53-gate terminal concourse at the Boone County airport, giving it the world's largest regional airline facility. The airline announced in 1998 a $40 million expansion of its airport headquarters, maintenance and training facilities, concourse, and corporate hangar.

▸ JIM CALLAWAY

The Northern Kentucky-based Comair has been so successful at redefining industry standards that many people no longer regard it as merely a regional airline. Rather, they appreciate what sets Comair apart from the average airline, and passenger boardings and the miles they log continue to increase substantially each year.

TENTE CASTERS, Inc.

IF IT HAS TO BE MOVED, IT OUGHT TO BE ON TENTE CASTERS. *That's the thinking at Hebron, Kentucky-based TENTE CASTERS, Inc., which makes and markets some 4,500 different types of casters, ranging in wheel size from one inch to 20 inches and ranging in load capacity per caster up to 10 tons. TENTE's slogan is, "We keep the world moving," and moving is precisely what it has* been doing since arriving on the scene more than two decades ago. Incorporated in September 1979, TENTE CASTERS celebrates 20 years with the Northern Kentucky community in 1999.

A caster is simply a wheel that's permanently mounted on a fork, which can be attached to a piece of equipment, thereby rendering the equipment movable instead of stationary. The basic design is simple in concept, but can be highly complex in detail. Casters come in all kinds of variations and combinations—fixed casters, swivel casters, locking casters, central-locking casters, single- and double-wheeled casters, swivel casters with directional locks, casters with plate fittings, casters with threaded-screw fittings, polyurethane-wheel casters, rubber-wheel casters, and many others.

Many of the most important innovations in caster design were created by TENTE CASTERS' parent, TENTE-ROLLEN GmbH & Co. of Wermelskirchen, Germany, near Cologne. Founded in June 1923 by Adolph Schulte, TENTE-ROLLEN started out making ball casters and sliding door casters for cupboards, but soon began broadening its product offerings with creatively engineered solutions to the problems created by all sorts of movable equipment.

An early innovation that marked TENTE as a pioneering industry leader was a patented system of central-locking casters that permits all four wheels to be locked simultaneously by moving a single lever. Such systems today can independently lock the directional swivel bearings on two or all four wheels, as well as lock the wheels or leave them free to roll—all by manipulating a single lever.

Applications of the company's products range from heavy industrial machinery to hospital beds and medical equipment to fine furniture and lightweight consumer products—virtually anything that has to be moved. TENTE has been awarded Germany's coveted Red Dot Award for Highest Design Quality, the Federal Award for Product Design, and the Golden Intrama Award at the international exposition in Brno.

The company has 10 subsidiaries around the globe, including the Hebron facility and others in Belgium, the Netherlands, England, South Africa, Ireland, France, the Czech Republic, Spain, and Leipzig, Germany. The privately held corporation has about 1,000 employees worldwide, including about 100 in Northern Kentucky.

Clockwise from top left:
Dr. Dietrich Fricke, president of TENTE CASTERS and longtime managing director of TENTE-ROLLEN, dedicated the Hebron, Kentucky, facility in May 1992.

Peter Fricke is following in his father's footsteps as managing director, leading the TENTE group into the new millennium.

Based in Hebron, TENTE CASTERS, Inc. makes and markets some 4,500 different types of casters, ranging in wheel size from one inch to 20 inches and ranging in load capacity per caster up to 10 tons.

Northern Kentucky Operations

In 1979, TENTE CASTERS began operations in Northern Kentucky as American TENTE CASTERS, Inc., under General Manager Horst Mende. Initially, the company was an importing and sales subsidiary with minor assembly operations. Its first offices were in Florence, but by 1982, the firm had outgrown this location. Subsequently, American TENTE CASTERS chose to build its own office space and factory in Erlanger.

After changing its name to TENTE CASTERS in January 1989, the company soon outgrew even its expanded facilities in Erlanger, prompting construction of a new, 44,000-square-foot complex at its present location in Hebron. In November 1991, operations began at Hebron, and the new facility was officially dedicated in May 1992 by Dr. Dietrich Fricke, president of TENTE CASTERS and longtime managing director of TENTE-ROLLEN.

The move to Hebron has allowed TENTE CASTERS to continue its strong pattern of growth. Bradford M. Hood, a Northern Kentucky native and a Beechwood High School graduate who joined the company's sales management team in 1988, succeeded Mende in 1993. The company received ISO 9002 certification in January 1996, a recognition of the company's tradition of high quality standards.

Further Expansion

Pressed by customer demands, TENTE CASTERS completed a new high-rise warehouse in May 1996 to store the thousands of parts to be assembled in making customized casters tailored to customers' precise needs and specifications. The warehouse enables TENTE to provide just-in-time deliveries to cost- and space-conscious equipment manufacturers.

In tandem with the warehouse expansion, which allows the company to inventory a greater variety of parts and assemblies imported from Germany, TENTE CASTERS has been expanding its in-house manufacturing capabilities. The company installed Cincinnati Milacron injection-molding equipment in the last few years, and now makes its own plastic wheels and other parts. This began as a two-shift operation, but quickly grew to three shifts per day.

In addition, TENTE CASTERS installed a new press for stamping and forming metal components, such as forks. This type of innovation is definitely the trend for the future: Making its own parts is not only less expensive, but also permits TENTE to shorten lead times, carry less inventory, and respond more nimbly to U.S. and Canadian customers. Under Dr. Fricke, TENTE has been a highly customer-driven company that stresses individualized service and the importance of building long-term relationships. Peter Fricke is following in his father's footsteps and leading the TENTE group into the new millennium.

Serving Diverse Industries

TENTE CASTERS supplies casters to a variety of industries in North America. Hospital bed makers and manufacturers of medical carts, stretchers, IV poles, EKG machines, and physical therapy equipment are among its biggest customers. Other uses include shopping carts, airplane food carts, television studio cameras, stage equipment, industrial equipment, office furniture, consumer products, retail fixtures, and tray racks/food warmers used in food-service operations.

Having celebrated its 75th anniversary in 1998, TENTE-ROLLEN is now closing in on eight decades of innovative leadership in the design and manufacture of casters worldwide. The company will continue this tradition as it rolls into the new millennium.

Clockwise from top:
Having celebrated its 75th anniversary in 1998, TENTE-ROLLEN GmbH & Co. of Wermelskirchen, Germany, is now closing in on eight decades of innovative leadership in the design and manufacture of casters worldwide.

TENTE CASTERS, Inc.'s production assembly facilities in Hebron, Kentucky, received ISO 9002 certification in January 1996.

Bradford M. Hood (left), a Northern Kentucky native and a Beechwood High School graduate, serves as managing director, while Rennie Beltramo is the vice president of operations.

O ONE HAS TO TELL THE PEOPLE AT MACKAY, INC. HOW *digital information technology is changing the way America works. For years, MacKay has been pushing the technology envelope at the forefront of an industry revolutionized by computerized graphics and advanced techniques for digital imagery manipulation.* ▣ *The company was founded by Robert MacKay in 1958 in* Louisville. In 1968, Minneapolis-based Bemis Company, Inc. acquired MacKay and, in 1981, created another branch, Gravure Systems Inc., at the company's present site on Empire Drive in Florence, Kentucky. Then as now, its purpose was to aggressively pursue new digital technologies and to apply them to graphic reproduction processes used in printing packaging. As the company's business flourished in Northern Kentucky, Bemis moved the Louisville operations in 1990 and consolidated them with Gravure Systems, renaming the entire organization MacKay, Inc.

Revolutionizing the Industry

Today, MacKay is helping to develop a less expensive, more efficient, and much more effective industry. As a leading supplier of graphics services to the packaged goods industry, the firm has transformed a business that was once driven by the hands-on work of skilled craftsmen into one based on increasingly sophisticated computer applications and digital file management systems. For instance, film, once the basic working medium for any graphic arts project, has been virtually eliminated from the process, except as an end product.

By combining the latest digital technology with traditional graphic arts techniques, MacKay can offer its customers the widest possible range of options while guaranteeing consistent high quality and reliability. Specializing exclusively in packaging, the company focuses all of its energies, experience, and talents on the unique applications required by its targeted customer base, thus anticipating their needs and staying ahead of the curve of fast-changing technology.

Providing Full Graphics Services

MacKay provides full graphics services for the three types of printing processes used by packaging printers for the consumer products industry: flexography, rotogravure, and offset lithography. Electronic scanners are used to transfer images from the customer's transparencies or reflective art into a digital format. MacKay also takes digital art and directly integrates it into its graphics systems. The resulting digital images can then be electronically retouched or manipulated in a number of ways to achieve whatever effects a customer may desire—all without corrupting the original image. Colorimetry and spectrophotometry are used to analyze and quantify characteristics such as hue, density, and chromatics so that colors are reproduced with extremely high precision. Digital color proofers then create filmless hard copies used for evaluation, fine-tuning, and, ultimately, customer approval.

CLOCKWISE FROM TOP:
THE MAIN PLANT AND CORPORATE OFFICES OF MACKAY, INC. ARE STRATEGICALLY LOCATED NEAR THE CINCINNATI/NORTHERN KENTUCKY INTERNATIONAL AIRPORT.

THE EXPOSING UNIT CREATES ONE OR MORE FILM IMAGES OF A PACKAGE OR LABEL FROM DIGITAL DATA. EXPOSURE TIME FOR A 42" X 63" SHEET OF FILM IS LESS THAN TWELVE MINUTES.

MACKAY USES PRECISE MEASURING DEVICES TO CONFIRM ENGRAVING SPECIFICATIONS REQUIRED BY HIGH-PRECISION GRAVURE CYLINDERS.

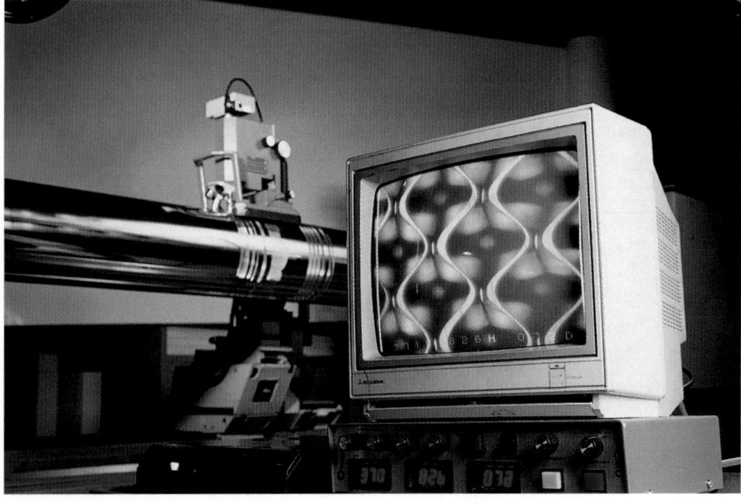

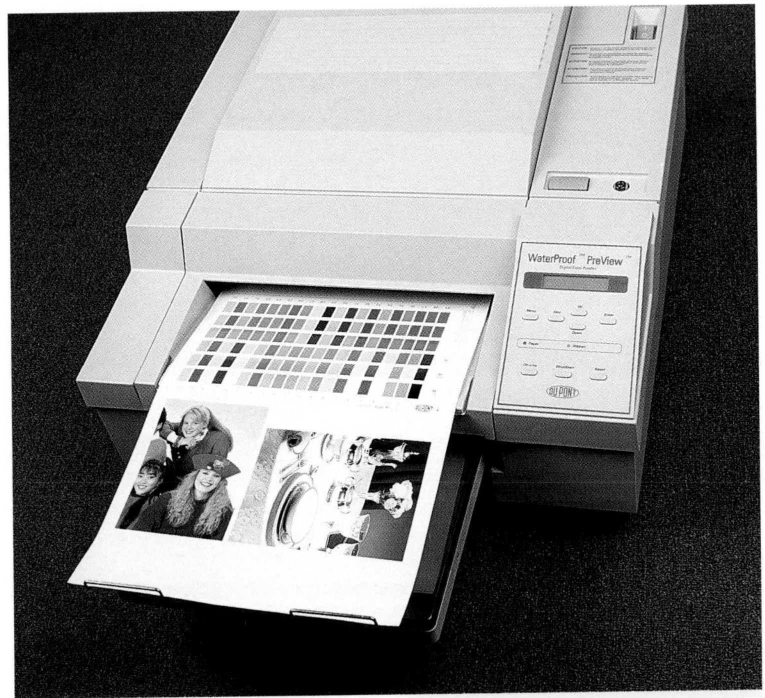

USING DIGITAL PROOFING DEVICES (TOP LEFT AND RIGHT), MACKAY IS CAPABLE OF PRODUCING HIGH-RESOLUTION IMAGES OF CUSTOMER ARTWORK.

EVALUATING PROOF DATA IS A WAY OF LIFE IN TODAY'S HIGH-TECH GRAPHICS WORLD, AND HIGHLY SOPHISTICATED EQUIPMENT IS A PREREQUISITE (BOTTOM).

By using the customer's own substrates and inks for proofing engraved cylinders or flexo plates, MacKay helps ensure that it will faithfully reproduce the original designs on actual production presses. The company supplies single-color and composite proofs for customer approval, which are then used to manufacture printed packaging and labeling from a variety of substrates.

MacKay's products are used to make packaging for food products, pet foods, beverages, baby supplies, and countless other goods. As a longtime leader in digital engraving, the firm is now applying its experience and technologies to more advanced graphics processes so it can service an even wider customer base.

Maintaining Total Quality

MacKay, Inc. works to maintain total quality at every step of the process, from inspection of incoming materials to the shipment of the finished products. The company's president, James A. Elliott, says, "Excellence is a habit at MacKay, not an accident. It's planned, programmed, and practiced daily by every person at the company."

MacKay has been ISO-9002 certified since 1996, one of the few suppliers of graphics services to achieve that high level of international quality assurance. According to Elliott, this is a firm that squarely faces up to the tough quality standards demanded by the global marketplace.

Anticipating New Technologies

In the time MacKay has operated in Northern Kentucky, the field of packaging graphics has evolved into an industry concerned with information handling, electronic file management, and the manipulation of digital graphic images. Today, the firm remains dedicated to anticipating tomorrow's technological trends, enabling it to develop cutting-edge systems to provide its customers with the highest-quality services and the widest range of options in the most convenient and accessible manner.

Technological innovation and new product development, as well as cooperation and quality assurance, are key corporate strategies at MacKay. As a global manufacturer of flexible packaging and pressure-sensitive materials, parent company Bemis penetrates new markets by bringing together the unique capabilities of its subsidiaries to meet customers' needs. From its Northern Kentucky base, MacKay plays a key role in that process by assuring that customers' graphic designs take full advantage of the exciting new possibilities in packaging and labeling.

Spartan Construction Inc.

SPARTAN CONSTRUCTION INC. IS A FAMILY FIRM THAT HAS *built its business from the ground up—literally. "We specialize primarily in underground construction," says Dianne Brossart, president of the Burlington, Kentucky-based company. "A lot of what we do you don't see. We put in drain tiles along expressways, and we do water and sewer work—anything related to underground infrastructure."*

Spartan was founded in 1982. With Dianne at the helm and sons Doug and Don now also active in the business, Spartan maintains a true family orientation. While the bulk of Spartan's business is located in Kentucky, the family-owned firm will travel throughout 13 states in the southeastern United States to meet the needs of its customers. Spartan is known primarily as a highway construction contractor and has developed a rapport with federal, state, and local governments. "Dealing with governments is probably better than working for anybody else," she maintains. "There's never any problem getting paid, and once you get to know the system, any bureaucracy is not too bad."

ONE OF SPARTAN CONSTRUCTION INC.'S MOST INTERESTING PROJECTS WAS THE RECENT CONSTRUCTION AND INSTALLATION OF THE ADVANCED REGIONAL TRAFFIC INTERACTIVE MANAGEMENT AND INFORMATION SYSTEM (ARTIMIS) ALONG 88 MILES OF FREEWAY AROUND GREATER CINCINNATI. THE JOB CONSISTED OF COMPLETING THE UNDERGROUND WORK AND LAYING FIBER OPTICS, INSTALLING CAMERAS, AND ERECTING SIGNAGE.

As part of its extensive government focus, Spartan has done most of the drainage work on major roadways from the Ohio River to Bowling Green, Kentucky. "We've worked almost all of Interstates 75, 65, and 71," adds Brossart. "I'd say that we've put in 90 percent of the drainage work on those roads in the state of Kentucky."

Spartan was also significantly involved in the construction of the new Delta Air Lines facility at the Cincinnati/Northern Kentucky International Airport, where the firm dug the tunnel for the train line between terminals.

One of Spartan's most interesting projects was its role in the recent construction and installation of the Advanced Regional Traffic Interactive Management and Information System (ARTIMIS) along 88 miles of freeway around Greater Cincinnati. The job consisted of completing the underground work and laying fiber optics, installing cameras, and erecting signage. The system, which consists of a complex network of sensors and cameras that relay information to a control center, lets drivers know about road emergencies immediately, whether it is a traffic problem or a smog alert. Spartan is currently planning to install a similar system in downtown Louisville.

Innovation Is the Key

During the course of its history, Spartan Construction has quickly established and refined a reputation for innovation. "Some time ago, the state of Kentucky added sewer and pipe inspection to their bids," says Brossart. "So we developed an underground system that incorporated onsite cameras linked with computers to do the inspection. We added our own elements to the system, and now we do practically all underground inspections for the state." The company has also patented numerous robotic elements of the system, making Spartan a leader in underground camera inspection technology.

"We like to think we cooperate with everyone," Brossart says. "We share technologies and develop-

SAYS DIANNE BROSSART, PRESIDENT OF THE BURLINGTON, KENTUCKY-BASED SPARTAN CONSTRUCTION INC., "A LOT OF WHAT WE DO YOU DON'T SEE. WE PUT IN DRAIN TILES ALONG EXPRESSWAYS, AND WE DO WATER AND SEWER WORK—ANYTHING RELATED TO UNDERGROUND INFRASTRUCTURE."

ments with other contractors so they can work with us on specific projects. I think that kind of cooperation develops a sense of camaraderie that you don't necessarily find everywhere, but I think it is somewhat common in our industry."

Spartan's ability to get along with customers and contractors is well established. Perhaps even more significant is Spartan's reputation in the business as the company to turn to when a job gets tough. "We specialize in difficult projects," Brossart says. "We'll go down as deep as 35 feet if that's what a job requires. Most other companies won't do that. We also have a very good safety record. And, frankly, since this is our specialty, we are one of the best in the business. The state of Kentucky will often call us for emergency work because they know we will get the job done safely."

Providing Jobs for Kentucky Families

While Spartan Construction actively bids for projects as far north as West Virginia and as far south as Florida, the company has recently concentrated its efforts in its home state, where there is currently a large volume of highway construction work. "We've been busy in Kentucky lately, and we like that," says Brossart. Presently, the firm is eager to secure more work on additional projects like the ARTIMIS system, which is rapidly becoming a Spartan specialty.

"We've done a lot of innovative work that most people won't tackle," says Brossart, "like rock trenching, which requires special equipment and experience. That is one of our specialties, but our bread and butter is highway work."

Spartan considers its large family of loyal employees to be its greatest asset and the true measure of its success. Explains Brossart, "We have lots of families that work for us. We have employees who are cousins or sons or brothers, and lots of these families have also sent their kids to work for us in the summers. So we are very proud of the fact that we have that kind of loyalty. It means we are a good company—and a good place to work."

Spartan is known primarily as a highway construction contractor and has developed a rapport with federal, state, and local governments.

TULIPS, WINDMILLS, WOODEN SHOES, AND RUBBER ROOFS? IN *most parts of the country, that last item doesn't evoke thoughts of Holland, but folks around Northern Kentucky have a somewhat different perspective. In these parts, Florence's Holland Roofing Group is fast becoming synonymous with rubber roofing for commercial structures of all types.* Wherever people go in Northern Kentucky and the Greater Cincinnati area, they may well find themselves sheltered under a roof by Holland Roofing. The company's commercial division has done it all: the huge Delta Air Lines terminal at the Cincinnati/Northern Kentucky International Airport, the Levi Strauss distribution center in Boone County that encompasses 18 acres under one roof, the fine sheet metal craftsmanship of the Oldenberg Brewery complex in Fort Mitchell, the Montgomery Inn Boathouse on the Cincinnati riverfront, and the innovative public aquarium in Newport.

The company regularly works on the biggest and most challenging projects in conjunction with virtually all of the area's major commercial developers, including Paul Hemmer Construction Co., Duke Realty Investments Inc., Industrial Developments International Inc., and Bunnell Hill Development Co. Since its founding in 1986, Holland Roofing has experienced phenomenal growth, particularly in recent years. Starting with 10 employees and first-year revenues of $1.8 million, the company now has nearly 200 employees and annual revenues in excess of $30 million.

A Winning Combination

In 1978, founder Hans Philippo immigrated to Northern Kentucky from his native Holland with his fiancée's family and his future father-in-law, Hugo DeVroomen. Since DeVroomen was in the tulip importing business, Philippo fully expected to make his living selling tulip bulbs. But he soon got sidetracked into roofing and jumped at an opportunity to start his own company. His father-in-law even assisted in lining up the financing.

Local real estate developers, distributors, and industrialists have profited from his decision, particularly since Philippo has kept his old-world traditions alive in the form of stringent European construction standards and a personal commitment to quality on projects of any size. Whether it's new construction, reroofing an existing building, or repairing a damaged roof, the company brings the same standard of excellence to the job. Because of Holland Roofing's size and organization, it has the flexibility to shift personnel and equipment to tackle jobs that others can't handle or can't get to quickly enough. In addition to its commercial roofing business, the company has a Northern Kentucky-based residential division.

Philippo, who serves as group president and chief executive officer, says success in the roofing business is a matter of quality workmanship, competitive pricing, and being able to start and complete a job quickly. He credits his company's superior organization and administration with giving it an edge on all three counts. Holland Roofing hires, trains, and promotes the best people in the trade, some of whom are now running regional offices in surrounding metropolitan markets such as Louisville; Columbus, Ohio; Indianapolis; Nashville; Atlanta; and Raleigh. The Nashville business, whose president started out as a sheet metal worker at Holland Roofing's home office in Florence, posted more than

HOLLAND ROOFING GROUP CONSISTENTLY EARNS SPECIAL RECOGNITION AND INDUSTRY AWARDS FOR OUTSTANDING VALUE, QUALITY, AND SAFETY ON PROJECTS THAT HAVE RANGED FROM MINOR REROOFING APPLICATIONS TO MORE THAN 10 ACRES IN NEW CONSTRUCTION.

▲▼ COURTESY OF M.A. THORNTON

▲▼ COURTESY OF M.A. THORNTON

$1 million in revenues in its first month of operation in 1997.

"It's not like they're working for me—they're working with me," Philippo says of his partners in the regional offices. Each owns a piece of the operation he oversees. All sales and administrative functions are handled in Florence, so the regional branches can concentrate on doing each job right and completing it quickly.

Industry Recognition

Much of Holland Roofing's work involves new buildings, and for developers as well as the businesses waiting to move in, time is money. "They know we have the manpower and the capacity to do it fast, so they call us," Philippo says, noting that Holland Roofing has been recognized as the 20th-largest roofing contractor in the United States by *Roofing, Siding, and Insulation*, a national trade magazine. By any measure, the company is the Northern Kentucky area's premier commercial roofing contractor.

Holland Roofing has been awarded the rubber roofing industry's highest honors from the two dominant manufacturers of roofing materials, Firestone and Carlisle SynTec Systems. As far as Philippo knows, his is the only roofing business in the country to have been so recognized by both. The company has received the Firestone Master Contractor Award, the Firestone Inner Circle of Quality Award, and most important, the Firestone President's Club Award. It is also one of very few roofing contractors inducted into the Carlisle SynTec Systems Hall of Fame. That exclusive award is the most respected honor in the industry, recognizing roofers who have completed at least 250 Perfect 10 jobs in the course of a year; Holland Roofing exceeded the minimum with 750 Perfect 10 applications. In addition, the company recently received Carlisle's award for Excellence in Single-Ply for the Midwest region of the United States.

The company plans to continue its aggressive expansion efforts into other markets in the years to come, capitalizing on the knowledge, experience, and industry contacts it has successfully assembled in Northern Kentucky. Thanks to that forward-looking approach, it's likely that Dutch windmills—at least the ones on the Holland Roofing Group's corporate logo—will be sighted with increasing frequency across the country.

Holland Roofing Group has had tremendous success with all types of projects throughout Northern Kentucky, including Chancellor Commons in Crestview Hills (left) and Merchants Square in Florence.

Holland Roofing Group is one of the industry's leading installers of commercial roofing products (left).

Only quality roofing products are installed by Holland's experienced and professional roof technicians (right).

▲▼ COURTESY OF M.A. THORNTON

A**S ANY BUSINESS OWNER OR COMPANY BENEFITS ADMINISTRATOR** *knows, group insurance is a serious matter. It's confusing enough by itself, but add the constant consolidation and restructuring in the insurance industry, and it can be almost incomprehensible. To effectively manage group insurance requires full-time attention, and Business Benefits, Inc. has that dedication.* George Beatrice started Business Benefits in 1984 in Fort Mitchell, Kentucky. Beatrice—then a 25-year veteran of the industry—turned down an executive promotion with a national life insurance carrier and decided it was time to start his own business and raise a family in Northern Kentucky. Today, Business Benefits, Inc. is the area's largest insurance agency that specializes in group insurance—group health, disability, dental, and life—as well as financial and retirement planning.

MICHAEL GURREN PHOTOGRAPHY

THE STAFF OF BUSINESS BENEFITS, INC. INCLUDES (STANDING, FROM LEFT) LEE ARKENAU, GERALYN ISLER, GEORGE BEATRICE, BOB BEATRICE, DAVE GEIS, PAM BERRY, (SEATED, FROM LEFT) JIM BEATRICE, GARY BEATRICE, TERRI JUSTICE, NANCY PAYNTER, AND TOM STEWART (NOT PICTURED).

As things have turned out, Beatrice not only kept the family in town, he was able to keep the business in the family. His three sons and two daughters now work with the thriving independent agency. One son, Gary, is not only president of the company, but a lawyer who's often sought out by legislators for his input on complex health insurance issues.

In addition to sales and marketing, son Jim designs and manages the in-house information systems; son Bob quickly established himself as one of the area's top agents upon joining the company in 1996; daughter Geralyn Isler is also an agent, and daughter Terri Justice researches and analyzes plans for large groups. The senior staff also includes nonfamily members Dave Geis, formerly with ChoiceCare, and financial planner Tom Stewart.

Servicing a Changing Market

The rapid pace of change in the insurance industry makes it nearly impossible for small businesses to know what's current in the market. It can be difficult for them to effectively negotiate with carriers or for their covered employees and their families to keep up with and fully understand the terms of their coverage.

"It's a market that's been undergoing tremendous upheaval, especially in Kentucky, where the law is changing dramatically in a lot of ways," says Gary Beatrice of the group health field. "Ten years ago, there were over 20 carriers writing policies in Northern Kentucky. Now there are six."

In the past, competitive pressures created by the sheer number of carriers trying to carve out a market share may have worked to businesses' advantage. Today, those same businesses need to hammer out the best possible terms individually—not merely to get the best price, but also to get the coverage that addresses their particular needs.

With more than 700 business clients in Northern Kentucky and Greater Cincinnati, Business Benefits has the necessary experience, industry clout, and broad market exposure to deliver for its clients. The company also has an extensive database and in-house information systems to steer clients and their covered employees through the maze of carriers, benefit designs, and procedures.

Amid the changes, Business Benefits continues to provide stability and accessibility. Rather than calling a carrier's 800 number on the West Coast and getting put on hold for 20 minutes, Business Benefits' clients can call and get immediate assistance from its service department, headed by Lee Arkenau, who is also the office manager and has been with the agency since its inception.

For convenient contact with the service and sales team, customers can call or visit the company's Web site at www.businessbenefits.com, which offers general services information and communication options.

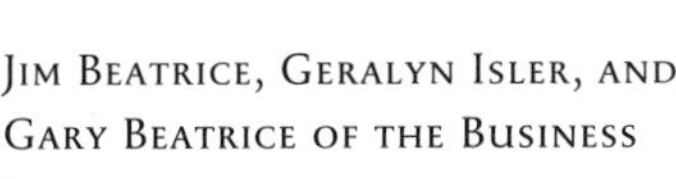

JIM BEATRICE, GERALYN ISLER, AND GARY BEATRICE OF THE BUSINESS BENEFITS SALES DEPARTMENT

MICHAEL GURREN PHOTOGRAPHY

To gauge the success experienced by the Tri-County *Economic Development Corporation of Northern Kentucky (Tri-ED) in barely a decade, one can simply look at the quality of the companies it's been instrumental in bringing to or expanding in the area—DHL Airways Inc.; Delta Air Lines; Heinz Pet Products and Star-Kist Foods, Inc.; Comair, Inc.; Fidelity Investments;* Levi Strauss & Company; Gibson Greetings, Inc.; The Gap/Banana Republic; Toyota Motor Manufacturing North America, Inc.; Sachs Automotive of America; Ashland, Inc.; GE Capital Information Technology Solutions—and the list goes on.

Tri-ED is typically the first organization in the area to establish contact with companies searching for office, manufacturing, and distribution sites. In addition, Tri-Ed has the critical task of ensuring that all parties involved—companies seeking sites, state and local government agencies, area corporations and business leaders, public utilities, and national and international location consultants—are moving in the same direction.

Created through Cooperation

The leaders at Tri-ED insist that the ongoing growth spurt in Northern Kentucky is the result of a communitywide partnership. Created as a nonprofit development corporation in 1987 by Boone, Kenton, and Campbell counties, Tri-ED is the primary economic development marketing agency for the three counties, blending public funds with private investment dollars to create jobs, tax revenue growth, and communitywide economic expansion. The services it provides the community are numerous: Tri-ED compiles demographic, economic, and labor market data; tracks available commercial and industrial sites and buildings; provides information on utilities, taxes, and transportation services; conducts economic impact and research studies; and provides referrals for local business support services.

From the beginning, Tri-ED has fostered a spirit of cooperation among diverse civic, government, and business groups that once competed but now see themselves as part of a team. Working together for the common good, these organizations are responsible for many outstanding accomplishments.
In the Tri-County Economic Development Corporation of Northern Kentucky's first 12 years, 251 industrial and service employers have created 27,339 new jobs and invested approximately $2.5 billion in Northern Kentucky. This has increased annual household earnings by nearly $2 billion. As a result, Tri-ED was recognized as one of the 10 best economic development organizations in the country by *Site Selection* magazine in 1995 and 1997, and again in 1998.

Long-Lasting Success

Beyond all the statistics, Tri-ED has created something more fundamental and long lasting in that it has helped to remake Northern Kentucky's image—locally, nationally, and even globally. Once viewed mostly as a collection of bedroom communities in the Cincinnati area, Northern Kentucky is now a full partner with its northern neighbor, economically and otherwise, and is highly regarded in its own right as home to hundreds of top-flight companies that ship their products around the world.

Scores of foreign companies—every one aggressively sought after by other communities across the Midwest and the nation—have looked, listened, and made all the complex calculations, and in the end, they have chosen Northern Kentucky as the best place to locate their U.S. operations. That's perhaps the most impressive measure of Tri-ED's success and a foundation on which it's building further successes for the future.

Clockwise from top:
In the Tri-County Economic Devlopment Corporation of Northern Kentucky's (Tri-ED) first 12 years, 251 industrial and service employers—such as Heinz Pet Products and Star-Kist Foods Inc., whose headquarters overlooks the Ohio River—have created 27,339 new jobs and invested approximately $2.5 billion in Northern Kentucky.

The Covington branch of Fidelity Investments, the nation's largest financial services provider, was one of Northern Kentucky and Tri-ED's first major companies.

In 1996, Toyota Motor Manufacturing North America, Inc. selected Northern Kentucky as the location of its North American manufacturing headquarters.

© GAIL KISSINGER

1988-1999

1988 David E. Estes Engineering, Inc.

1988 NS Group, Inc.

1991 CenterBrain International, Inc.

1992 The Northern Kentucky Symphony

1992 Willamette Industries Preprint Plant

1992 WNKR Mix 106.5 FM

1994 SpanPro, Inc.

1996 Toyota Motor Manufacturing
North America, Inc. (TMMNA)

1998 Northern Kentucky
Convention Center Corporation

1998 WILD Flavors, Inc.

1999 Ashland Inc.

1999 GE Capital IT Solutions

David E. Estes Engineering, Inc.

SINCE ITS INCEPTION IN 1988, DAVID E. ESTES ENGINEERING, *Inc. has grown to become one of the most recognized civil engineering, environmental consultation, and land-surveying firms in the Greater Cincinnati/Northern Kentucky area. Headquartered in Florence, Kentucky, Estes started with six employees, but has since grown to a staff of 40 employees and has* added a full-service office in Cincinnati.

With more than 1,200 projects completed in its first 10 years, Estes believes its high percentage of repeat business directly correlates with the high quality of its work product. Client satisfaction translates into repeat business, and client loyalty is a result of Estes' commitment to effective, economical, and responsive professional service.

Members of the Estes team have been specifically chosen for their technical ability, professionalism, experience, and ethics. Together, these individuals bring to the company more than 150 years of valuable experience, which they gained through working with other consulting firms, government agencies, and private industry. Project assignments are made based on each individual's background, work schedule, training, and pertinent experience. Their familiarity with local, state, and federal requirements keeps projects on target and within budget.

Civil Engineering Division

Estes is able to offer a wide range of services through its three major divisions. The Civil Engineering Division concentrates on commercial centers, industrial sites, residential subdivisions, streets and highways, and aviation facilities, as well as water and storm/sanitary sewer systems. With extensive experience in transportation, developmental, and infrastructure engineering, members of this team include President and Principal Engineer David E. Estes, P.E., L.S., as well as senior engineers, project managers, field engineers, and computer aided design and drafting (CADD) technicians. The CADD team consists of technicians who have numerous years of design experience and technical drafting skills. Estes uses the most current version of AUTOCADD to provide drawings to match its clients' requirements.

Surveying Division

The Surveying Division includes licensed surveyors and multiple field teams that can handle any surveying and siting work and provide precision control, boundary resolution, topographic mapping, and Cadastral and ALTA/ACSM land title surveys. The company has invested in satellite-based global positioning technology (GPS), and routinely uses Trimble GPS Total Station 4000 SSI as well as TRIMMAP GPSurvey software for post processing and mapping of both GPS and conventional survey data.

Environmental Division

Estes Environmental Division offers a full range of services, from Phase I and II Environmental Site Assessments to groundwater and soil investigations to compliance audits to developing environmental management programs. With many years of geological, biological, chemical, and engineering experience in consultation, industry, training, and research, the team is familiar with the regulatory requirements in this geographical region, and it studies future regulatory trends to determine how these regulations can be approached to both enhance economic development and protect the environment.

The Estes Engineering mission is to set the standard for excellence in providing professional service through cost-effective design solutions by exceeding the clients' expectations for professional performance and technical competence, and by using the latest technology, such as the Internet—Estes' details its many services at www.estesengineering.com. David E. Estes himself is committed to expanding the firm into the new millennium by continually seeking new engineering opportunities and challenges and by proactively pursuing their appropriate solutions.

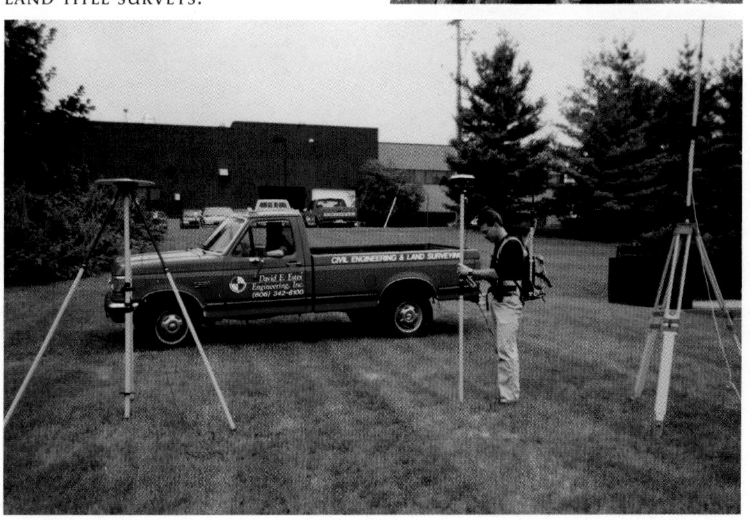

CLOCKWISE FROM TOP:
DAVID E. ESTES ENGINEERING, INC.'S CIVIL ENGINEERING DIVISION CONCENTRATES ON COMMERCIAL CENTERS, INDUSTRIAL SITES, RESIDENTIAL SUBDIVISIONS, STREETS AND HIGHWAYS, AND AVIATION FACILITIES, AS WELL AS WATER AND STORM/SANITARY SEWER SYSTEMS. IT ALSO SPECIALIZES IN ENVIRONMENTAL SERVICES, SUCH AS THIS CONFINED-SPACE ENTRY AND CLEANING PROJECT FOR AN AUTOMOBILE DEALERSHIP.

ESTES' FAMILIARITY WITH LOCAL, STATE, AND FEDERAL REQUIREMENTS KEEPS PROJECTS ON TARGET AND WITHIN BUDGET. THIS QUALITY HELPED TO MAKE THE DELTA AIR LINES EXPANSION PROJECT AT CINCINNATI/NORTHERN KENTUCKY INTERNATIONAL AIRPORT A SUCCESS.

THE ESTES SURVEYING DIVISION USES SATELLITE-BASED GLOBAL POSITIONING TECHNOLOGY AND CAN HANDLE ANY SURVEYING AND SITING WORK, PROVIDING PRECISION CONTROL, BOUNDARY RESOLUTION, TOPOGRAPHIC MAPPING, AND CADASTRAL AND ALTA/ACSM LAND TITLE SURVEYS.

Willamette Industries Preprint Plant

ACCORDING TO MULTIPLE INDUSTRY SOURCES, NEARLY 54 PERCENT *of impulse purchases are influenced by product packaging. Knowing the importance of great-looking design, Willamette Industries Preprint Plant realizes that while consumers are more sophisticated today than ever before, cutting through the clutter of so many competing products often comes down to the packaging. The ability* to provide manufacturers with attractive, yet cost-effective designs has allowed Willamette to carve a significant niche in the packaging industry.

The preprint plant is a division of the Portland, Oregon-based Willamette Industries, Inc., a vertically integrated forest products corporation that specializes in value-added wood products and building materials, as well as containerboard, corrugated box products, and cut-sheet paper. The company owns more than 1.7 million acres of timberland in the South and Pacific Northwest, and maintains more than 100 manufacturing facilities in the United States, Europe, and Mexico.

With Northern Kentucky operations in Richwood since 1992, Willamette is a flexographic printing firm that produces top-quality preprinted packaging materials for a wide range of industries. Its leaders point to several trends in product packaging that have helped build the business of this specialty printer. One such trend involves the desire to communicate as much information as possible to the consumer at the point of purchase. In response, Willamette strives to accommodate all the necessary information in an attractive, highly graphic format right on the package.

One of the Best Sales Tools Available

Utilizing a highly sophisticated mix of graphic design solutions, innovative prepress equipment, state-of-the-art plating techniques, and computer-assisted color matching, Willamette is able to offer high-volume flexographic printing for some of the world's largest consumer materials producers. The company's unique system allows manufacturers to display information in attractive formats, using varnished finishes and up to six colors. Ultimately, these capabilities contribute to a high-gloss package that actually becomes one of the best sales tools available for a manufacturer.

Beginning with a world-class graphics department, Willamette designs marketing materials from scratch, and works with advertising and design agencies to devise a package that will catch the consumer's eye. The company's computer-aided design equipment is fully integrated into its production departments, providing for more accurate and more dynamic artwork.

Willamette's ink lab is one of the best in the industry. Staff chemists use the latest computer technology to develop inks that provide fresher, cleaner color matching, and all of the laminates used by the company are water based for easier breakdown. In short, Willamette can fulfill virtually any color request to exacting detail.

At one time, packaging of this type could only be postprinted, which severely limited the graphics that could be used. By printing directly onto the linerboard before it is combined with the corrugated medium to form the containerboard, Willamette has helped to revolutionize the packaging industry. The company's large-scale platemaking capabilities provide greater flexibility for clients, allowing them to use more of the package's surface area for graphic elements and design. The large-format plate, manufactured from a resilient and pliable material, allows Willamette to run faster, more effective jobs for customers, and helps to raise quality and cut overall costs.

Finally, when the job is on the press, the company is able to offer the best in printing for corrugated box applications. This preprinting approach also enhances overall strength, protecting products better than if the packaging is produced by direct printing or utilizing offset labels. At Willamette, the result is colorful, informative packaging that helps grab consumers' attention and sell more products.

Willamette Industries Preprint Plant's unique printing system allows manufacturers to display information in attractive formats, using varnished finishes and up to six colors. Ultimately, these capabilities contribute to a high-gloss package that actually becomes one of the best sales tools available for a manufacturer (top right).

Clockwise from top: After developing a client's graphics in its film preparation and printing plate department, Willamette then preprints the linerboard using a six-color flexographic press. Next, the linerboard is gathered into finished preprint rolls before being formed into corrugated sheets. This unique preprinting system allows for more complicated, more dynamic graphics.

NORTHERN KENTUCKY'S NEWPORT IS A SMALL OHIO RIVER CITY, *perhaps best known for an infamous past that includes gambling, organized crime, and a bustling nightclub district. But located between the river and the streets of the city's row house district is the headquarters of NS Group, Inc., which represents another part of Newport's history—its steelmaking industry.* NS Group is primarily a leading specialty steel producer for the energy industry. Though only 18 years old, the company can trace its roots back to an industry that started in Newport in the mid-1800s. In years past, the massive Newport Steel Works made flat-rolled steel and sheets of steel from a 33-acre plant that employed, at times, up to 3,000 people.

A Shift in Ownership

When Clifford R. Borland arrived at the Newport Steel Works in 1977 as the new plant manager, the facility was plagued by antiquated equipment and a history of unprofitability. Borland ran the operation for only three years before it faced a crisis that would lead to its shutdown and to its eventual rebirth. At odds with organized labor over contract negotiations, the plant's owner, Interlake Inc., delivered an ultimatum to the union—accept the final offer or the mill would be closed. In July 1980, Interlake made good on its threat and ceased operations in Newport and in nearby Wilder, Kentucky, leaving 1,100 steelworkers unemployed.

Borland and a group of other managers saw opportunity in the misfortune. They quickly devised a plan to buy the shuttered steel operations. "We just got a wild idea that it might be possible to purchase the plants," Borland recalls, "but we had no idea how we were going to pull it off."

It took eight months of negotiations and attempts to raise the money needed to buy the plants. "We asked for help from anybody and everybody we could think of," Borland says. The group's diligence paid off; in April 1981, after securing financing commitments from the State of Kentucky, the federal government, local bankers, and even the seller, four former Interlake managers successfully acquired the operations. "People at Interlake recognized there was far greater value in selling the plants to us than scrapping them," Borland says.

A New Beginning

Borland, a Pennsylvania native trained as a metallurgical engineer, suddenly found himself at the helm of a reborn company with a promising start. The new owners hired back several hundred workers and concentrated solely on producing "oil country tubular goods"—tubular steel products used primarily in oil and natural gas drilling and production.

At the time, the demand for tubular steel was strong, and NS Group had commitments for one year's worth of production before it even started up. The tide soon turned for the new company, however, when a recession hit in early 1982 and demand sharply diminished.

"We were fortunate that we only had eight months under our belts," Borland recalls, "because we hadn't gotten fat, dumb, and happy yet. We quickly made every necessary move to get through a pretty serious recession."

CLIFFORD R. BORLAND IS CHAIRMAN, PRESIDENT, AND CHIEF EXECUTIVE OFFICER OF NS GROUP, INC. (RIGHT).

A NEW, $25 MILLION, ELECTRIC ARC FURNACE AT THE NEWPORT FACILITY IS CAPABLE OF PRODUCING APPROXIMATELY 750,000 TONS OF STEEL PER YEAR AND WILL SIGNIFICANTLY REDUCE PRODUCTION COSTS (LEFT).

A new, 16-inch cage roll forming system at the Newport facility expands NS Group's product size range and reduces costs.

The company survived and went on to purchase several other steelmaking plants, some of which had also been shut down because of labor problems. As it reinvested earnings into new equipment in Wilder and gained other operations through acquisition, what began as a single, fledgling pipe mill became a significant minimill operation.

In 1990, NS Group bought Koppel Steel, another closed plant in western Pennsylvania. That acquisition took the company into the seamless tube business, as well as special bar quality products, which are used for warehousing, forging, and automotive applications. In 1986, NS Group bought Erlanger Tubular Corp., a pipe-finishing plant near Tulsa, where the company now processes and finishes a portion of its welded and seamless tubular steel. In 1985, with an eye toward diversification, the company also purchased Cincinnati-based Imperial Adhesives Inc., which produces adhesives for a multitude of applications.

Going Public

A major turning point for NS Group occurred in 1988, when an initial public offering raised more than $45 million in equity. Although the company's stock was initially traded on the American Stock Exchange, it is now listed on the New York Stock Exchange under the symbol NSS.

As a supplier to the volatile energy industry, NS Group realizes that its fortunes are heavily tied into world demand for oil and other economic conditions. "We have to be a lot more flexible than most companies in manufacturing because of the highly cyclical nature of our business," Borland says.

To increase its financial flexibility and help insulate the company from recession, NS Group completed a successful secondary common stock offering in 1997, which sold 6 million shares for net proceeds of $170 million. The money raised will enable the company to invest $100 million in its plants over the next three years. In addition, NS Group reported its best year ever in 1997, when it achieved record profits, record shipments, and sales of nearly $500 million.

Two of the original four managers who bought out the company remain active today—Borland, NS Group chairman and chief executive officer, and Ronald Noel, president of the Newport Steel unit. Says Borland, "We built it all from nothing in 1981, and I think we're in a better position today than we ever have been in the past."

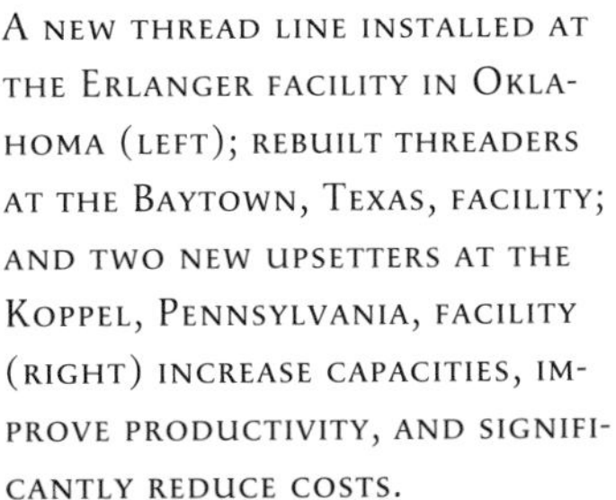

A new thread line installed at the Erlanger facility in Oklahoma (left); rebuilt threaders at the Baytown, Texas, facility; and two new upsetters at the Koppel, Pennsylvania, facility (right) increase capacities, improve productivity, and significantly reduce costs.

CenterBrain International, Inc.

STRATEGIC CONSULTING FIRMS ARE MADE UP OF LEFT-BRAINED *people who help companies develop strategies. Advertising agencies are made up of right-brained people who help companies put art behind their strategies. Although the two seldom work hand in hand, CenterBrain International, Inc. helps span the gap between the left- and right-brained thinkers. The company's focus is on* melding strategy and creativity into a coherent, efficient, whole-brained positioning agency to help businesses grow.

"The creative element is here," says Jim Ebel, founder and president of CenterBrain. "But all the creative people at our company are grounded in the pragmatics of business. That's the CenterBrain idea: the left and right brains coming together."

So far this approach has worked wonders for the company. Since its founding in 1991, CenterBrain has grown steadily. After opening satellite offices in New York and Chicago in 1997, the company expanded to new headquarters in Covington a year later.

"We've put more than $1 billion worth of new business on the market for our clients over the past seven years," says Ebel. "We have a 95 percent client return rate, and those clients who come back stay with us for a long time." CenterBrain's client list is a blue-chip roster that includes Fruit of the Loom, Kimberly-Clark Corp., Abbott Laboratories, Reynolds Metals, Heinz, Starkist, Bridgestone/Firestone, and Anheuser-Busch.

JIM EBEL (FAR LEFT), FOUNDER AND PRESIDENT OF CENTERBRAIN INTERNATIONAL, INC.; MIDNIGHT, THE COMPANY'S MASCOT; AND THE CINCINNATI CENTERBRAIN STAFF ALL FOCUS ON MELDING STRATEGY AND CREATIVITY—THE RIGHT AND LEFT SIDES OF THE BRAIN—INTO A COHERENT, EFFICIENT, AND WHOLE-BRAINED POSITIONING AGENCY.

"THE CREATIVE ELEMENT IS HERE," SAYS EBEL, "BUT ALL THE CREATIVE PEOPLE AT OUR COMPANY ARE GROUNDED IN THE PRAGMATICS OF BUSINESS. THAT'S THE CENTERBRAIN IDEA: THE LEFT AND RIGHT BRAINS COMING TOGETHER."

A Unique Concept

CenterBrain's unique positioning agency concept was born from Ebel's years of experience in the packaged goods business, working for such companies as Kimberly-Clark, Bristol-Myers Squibb Company, and Iams Company.

"What companies traditionally have been good at is knowing what to make and how to make it well. In addition, these companies have some critical mass in marketing and systems in place for distributing the products," Ebel says. "The missing piece I saw—and why companies seem to fail so often—is that they weren't communicating something meaningful to the consumer, and they weren't communicating it in a precise way that was unique and compelling."

In an attempt to solve this positioning problem, companies turn to advertising agencies, strategic consultants, and market research firms. However, each area offers at best only a piece of the puzzle. CenterBrain applies all three disciplines at the same time; the company calls it the Triad Process™.

"What makes us different from strategic consultants and advertising agencies is that we have found a way to truly apply the left and right brain thinking simultaeously," Ebel says. "That simultaneous thinking is driven by stimuli we receive from consumers. We also bring in an element of market research. Ultimately, what makes us different is how we think. The process itself—the Triad Process—is what gets our clients so excited."

The results get the clients excited, too. For example, CenterBrain developed advertising copy for the Fruit of the Loom women's underwear line that doubled retail purchase intent. Consequently, the company's campaign doubled sales for the underwear line in 1994.

"I've seen the Triad Process work in a lot of different categories," says Peter Gonze, vice president of Boston-based MediSense, a division of Abbott Laboratories, who has worked with Ebel on marketing Fact Plus® pregnancy tests and a line of products for diabetics. "What Ebel and CenterBrain deliver is a high-quality product."

As CenterBrain International, Inc. continues to bring the left and right brains together, clients will continue to get the best of both worlds. The result is a marketing approach that is both successful and unique.

In 1992, the Northern Kentucky Symphony (NKS) was *founded to open the door for a new audience to enjoy classical music. While traditionalists scoffed, the NKS experienced remarkable growth. By the summer of 1996, the American Symphony Orchestra League had recognized the NKS as the fastest-growing orchestra in America. Artistic vision, annual balanced budgets,* and strong management have combined to provide Northern Kentucky with a major cultural asset.

The NKS' mission differs from traditional orchestras much like General Motors differs from high-priced imports. Offering a wide variety of musical styles, NKS concerts appeal to a broader, younger market with high quality and value. "Programming is our product," says James Cassidy, the orchestra's founding music and executive director. "Symphonic music should enrich, educate, and entertain. At the same time, it has to be packaged and presented in a way to make the art attractive, accessible, and affordable."

Each NKS program is fashioned around an intriguing theme to provide a context for the listener, as well as fresh marketing appeal. Incorporating extramusical ideas also helps to dispel the notion that classical music must be elitist or intimidating. The NKS has greeted its audiences with mounted Civil War cavalry officers and cannons ("The War between the States"/ Fifth Ohio Light Artillery), astronomical displays ("The Final Frontier"/Cincinnati Observatory Center), aerobics instructors ("Sweatin' to the Symphony"), board games ("Trivial Pursuits"/ Hasbro), and pop culture videos ("Deep Thoughts"/NBC's *Saturday Night Live*). Guest artists have included Metropolitan Opera regulars, media personalities, and alternative and country bands. Concertgoers can find events calendars and symphony news at the NKS home page, located at www.nkso.org.

In recent years, smaller subsidiary groups have helped the NKS expand its reach. The Newport Ragtime Band (ragtime and early jazz), SouthBank Theatre Orchestra (light classics and vintage scores), New Crosley Square Orchestra (big band), SouthBank Chorale (NKS chorus), and a brass quintet have added variety and artistic flexibility while serving as ambassadors for both the orchestra and the community.

Among its most important offerings is the NKS' comprehensive education series. Elementary, middle, and high school students attend free concerts that introduce the instruments of the orchestra, explain the historical development of the orchestra and its music, and demonstrate how classical music continues to play a part in people's daily lives. Groups and individual musicians also travel to area schools for performances and clinics.

With offices in Newport, the NKS performs throughout the year in many locations. Greaves Concert Hall is home to five pairs of subscription concerts and 10 education performances. A series of four summer programs brings thousands of people to the amphitheater at Devou Park. Run-out concerts and special events also take the NKS to a number of cities and communities throughout the Tri-State.

The NKS' future remains linked to its creative marketing, artistic integrity, and personal connection with its audience. Televised performances, statewide tours, expanded community and education outreach, and the possible construction of a regional performing arts center will greatly enhance the Northern Kentucky Symphony's role locally and throughout the commonwealth.

Wielding a fresh and innovative approach to both programming and marketing, Music/Executive Director James Cassidy offers the following tip: "The NKS—Bet to win!" (left).

A student attending one of the NKS Education Concerts asks the conductor, "Why do you shake that violin player's hand?" (right).

The NKS presents "Sweatin' to the Symphony"—an aerobics class and concert in one (top).

The Northern Kentucky Symphony cello section celebrates George Gershwin's 100th birthday (left).

ORTHERN KENTUCKY NEWS, SPORTS, TRAFFIC, AND THE *hottest kickin' country have only one place they all call home—WNKR Mix 106.5 FM.* *Not many years ago, it was almost impossible for people living in Northern Kentucky to find out what was happening each day in their community or even their own state. And when it came to Northern Kentucky traffic delays, school* closings, and sports updates, they would be announced at the tail end of a Cincinnati newscast—if at all.

But that changed in April 1992 when WNKR radio—Mix 106.5—arrived on the scene with its pledge to provide the area's listeners with the most comprehensive Northern Kentucky coverage possible. At WNKR, this concept starts right at the top. The station is locally owned and operated by Grant County Broadcasters, Inc., with studios in Dry Ridge.

News, Closings, Weather, and Traffic

When Northern Kentuckians tune in, they notice things are done a little differently at WNKR. The station targets nine counties—Boone, Bracken, Campbell, Gallatin, Grant, Harrison, Kenton, Owen, and Pendleton—as its primary market. But its focus on these counties doesn't come at the expense of Cincinnati news. WNKR has a Cincinnati news bureau and reports many Cincinnati stories that affect Northern Kentucky—but only after completely covering Northern Kentucky news. WNKR's news team is one of the most experienced in the Tri-State area. When news happens in Northern Kentucky, WNKR reports it first.

That's also where WNKR puts its school closings: first in all newscasts and then every 15 minutes thereafter. While Cincinnati stations typically run through all Ohio closings before those in Southeast Indiana and Northern Kentucky, WNKR limits its coverage exclusively to Northern Kentucky schools, so listeners don't have to wade through a long list of out-of-state closings and can quickly learn if their children's school is closed.

WNKR also customizes weather and traffic reports just for Northern Kentucky. Weather conditions

KEVIN BRUMMER

KEVIN BRUMMER

LISTENERS KNOW THAT THE N-K-R IN WNKR MIX 106.5 FM STANDS FOR NORTHERN KENTUCKY RADIO. UNDER THE OWNERSHIP OF (FROM LEFT) RON LAWSON, NICOLE SIMPSON, AND ROBERT WALLACE, SERVING NORTHERN KENTUCKY RESIDENTS AND BUSINESSES IS WHAT WNKR DOES BEST (TOP).

WNKR TARGETS NORTHERN KENTUCKY AS ITS PRIMARY AUDIENCE, OFFERING LISTENERS LOCAL NEWS AND UPDATES (BOTTOM).

can vary dramatically from one end of town to the other; parts of Northern Kentucky often get slammed by storms that leave Cincinnati untouched. That's why listeners turn to chief meteorologist Tom Burse in WNKR's exclusive Northern Kentucky Weather Center for complete and accurate weather coverage. Likewise, traffic snarls don't simply end at the I-75 cut in the hill. WNKR's policy of "Northern Kentucky and only Northern Kentucky traffic" keeps listeners traveling smoothly from Covington to Corinth.

Kickin' Country

Of course, any radio station calling itself Kickin' Country Mix 106.5 is much more than news, school closings, weather, and traffic. WNKR broadcasts in stereo 24 hours a day, kickin' out the best contemporary country music from Nashville's hottest superstars. Spinning the hits is an announcer staff that knows Northern Kentucky inside and out. Mornings are anchored by Jay Anthony, who has an extensive, 13-year country radio background. WNKR's Larry B hosts afternoons from 2 to 7. And if that name sounds familiar, it should: Larry B, a Northern Kentucky resident, is the Tri-State's most recognized country disc jockey, with more than 25 years of broadcasting experience in this area alone. Other WNKR personalities include Penny Mitchell during midday, Bobby Sherman and Joani Williams in the evening, and Bill Saul overnight.

WNKR makes weekends extra special with free music giveaways, listener requests, and enough sports to keep even the most avid enthusiast satisfied. WNKR has exclusive Northern Kentucky rights to broadcast the University of Kentucky (UK) Wildcats basketball and football. In addition, the station carries all the related pregame and postgame interviews, as well as UK talk shows such as *The Big Blue Line* and *BenchTalk*. To say the station bleeds blue would be an understatement. Since 1992, WNKR has celebrated over the airwaves seven Southeastern Conference tournament titles, two NCAA national championships, and two bowl appearances.

NASCAR racing is America's fastest growing sport, and WNKR's listeners are guaranteed a front row seat by their radio for all Winston Cup, Busch, and Craftsman Truck races. The Brickyard 400 and the Indianapolis 500 are also covered. With a brand-new race track opening soon in nearby Sparta, WNKR is the station of choice for thousands of area racing enthusiasts who enjoy this exciting, fast-paced sport.

Since WNKR targets some 400,000 listeners in Northern Kentucky alone, businesses seeking a customer base in the state quickly see the benefits of advertising with the station. By comparison, nearly 70 percent of all Cincinnati radio station listeners reside in Ohio or Indiana, and very few of them venture into Kentucky to shop or locate consumer services. When businesses advertise on WNKR, they realize they are reaching a large number of potential Northern Kentucky customers.

Listeners know that the N-K-R in WNKR stands for Northern Kentucky radio. Serving Northern Kentucky residents and businesses is what WNKR Mix 106.5 FM does best.

▲ Amanda Cox

▲ Amanda Cox

The WNKR live broadcast ensemble includes a fully equipped van and an eye-catching broadcasting tent (top).

Larry B, a Northern Kentucky resident and the area's most recognized country disc jockey, plays the best in country music afternoons from 2 to 7 (bottom).

THE TELECOMMUNICATIONS FIELD IS EXPLODING, AND A LOCAL *company is expanding along with it. SpanPro, Inc., a Florence, Kentucky-based corporation that services every facet of telecommunications for a growing list of clients nationwide, has witnessed an impressive 2,000 percent net revenue growth since 1995. Begun in 1994 with two employees, SpanPro now has more than* 200 employees and more than 105 years of telecommunications experience among its senior management. Business opportunities are surging for this enterprise as companies continue to enter and expand in the highly promising telecommunications field.

A single, proven resource providing a multitude of services, SpanPro is well positioned to serve this growing market. Among its services are field mapping, computer-aided design and drafting (CADD), design of broadband communication systems, global positioning system (GPS) surveys and mapping, geographical information systems (GIS), a full range of fiber-optic design and installation services, line construction and maintenance, and custom software development.

Serving an industry as competitive and performance-driven as telecommunications is a constant challenge. SpanPro has combined the latest technologies with superior service to meet the demands of the marketplace. It also focuses on careful management of projects, ensuring work is performed to the highest standards and to the complete satisfaction of the customer.

A Florence, Kentucky-based corporation that services every facet of telecommunications for a growing list of clients nationwide, SpanPro, Inc. has witnessed an impressive 2,000 percent net revenue growth since 1995. With proven success behind it and opportunities ahead, SpanPro is on the cutting edge of technology and is poised to move boldly into the next century.

Five Customer-Focused Companies

SpanPro responds to customers' varying needs with the strategically focused skills and expertise of its five separate companies. The companies—SpanPro, Inc., SpanPro Fiber Optics, Inc., SpanPro GPS, SpanPro Solutions, and SpanPro Electrical—are integrated, yet operate as stand-alone businesses. Each prides itself on providing unique, superior services delivered in the most timely and cost-efficient manner. The integrated format allows and encourages information sharing among the staffs of the five companies, enhancing SpanPro's overall performance. It enables customers to quickly access just those services required to meet their most specific needs. And it provides SpanPro the flexibility to expand and form new synergies in the marketplace as opportunities arise.

SpanPro, Inc., the core division, works with customers such as MediaOne, Time Warner Inc., and Adelphia Communications, all leading providers of cable TV services, assisting them in the design of system upgrades. SpanPro first performs a field survey to assess the situation. Then, draftsmen use computer-assisted design (CAD) to create initial plans. From here, SpanPro designers use the information to develop a telecommunications system at the specific level requested.

SpanPro GPS grew out of SpanPro's work with utility companies. Using its global positioning system capabilities to help utility companies inventory their plants,

Traveling on the trade show circuit, SpanPro, Inc. most recently exhibited its family of resources and services at the 1999 Cable Tec Expo in Orlando, Florida, and plans to attend the Cable Tec Expo again in the year 2000, when it is held in Las Vegas, Nevada.

SpanPro founders realized GPS had far-reaching applications, especially within the telecommunications world. They began using GPS as part of a research project, which paid off so handsomely that SpanPro GPS now uses global positioning satellites to quickly and accurately map geographic territories and locate specific targets within territories for its clients. For instance, the company assists the U.S. Bureau of Alcohol, Tobacco and Firearms (ATF) in the difficult search for hazardous materials on sites that are enveloped in hilly terrain.

SpanPro Solutions, the firm's software development division, also stemmed from its core business. SpanPro found that many of its customers had made a serious investment in software, but were not getting the kind of results they expected. The firm saw the opportunity to help these businesses run a more efficient, profitable organization by writing new software for their particular needs or by modifying their existing programs. Today, SpanPro computer experts maximize current technologies within customers' organizations, helping them achieve optimal value for their software investment. The SpanPro Solutions team specializes in building customized programs to help clients achieve and maintain the highest efficiency level possible through both administrative and production tools.

Serving clients in Ohio, Michigan, Tennessee, Texas, Pennsylvania, Wisconsin, Kentucky, and Indiana, SpanPro Fiber Optics, Inc. provides the full spectrum of services required to develop today's advanced telecommunications systems. A highly versatile organization, SpanPro Fiber Optics, Inc. installs local area networks and wide area networks, and handles everything from design and installation to ongoing maintenance and emergency restoration. The group stands out as a single source supplier, providing the in-house talent, advanced systems equipment, and leading-edge processes to support customers' goals and growth demands. Its comprehensive services are available individually or as a turnkey operation, and the company is setting a new standard in customer satisfaction.

SpanPro Electrical is also an integral part of SpanPro's operations. It offers a wide range of residential and commercial wiring capabilities, including design, installation, and service. Typical customer requests include emergency repair, renovation and rewiring, service upgrades, installation of wiring and cabling for computers, backup electrical systems, fire alarm and security system wiring, and preventive maintenance. Licensed, trained, and bonded electrical experts deliver prompt and professional service throughout the Greater Cincinnati area via radio-dispatched service trucks. The company is recognized for its knowledgeable, reliable workmanship at reasonable rates.

An Investment in People

One of SpanPro's greatest strengths is that 90 percent of the work it does is performed by its own employees, not subcontractors. The company has invested heavily in training and has deliberately sought out quality people to serve its clients and build its business. The company's philosophy includes making certain its employees have a sense of ownership in the products and service they deliver. SpanPro encourages and supports continuing education for all employees, and offers and assumes the cost for cross-training and supplemental training programs.

SpanPro sees the enormous growth of the Internet, the bandwidth explosion, and other activity in the telecommunications industry as reason to believe its own growth will continue at above average levels. With proven success behind it and opportunities ahead, SpanPro is poised to move boldly into the next century.

A highly versatile organization, SpanPro Fiber Optics, Inc. installs local area networks and wide area networks, and handles everything from design and installation to ongoing maintenance and emergency restoration.

Toyota Motor Manufacturing North America, Inc. (TMMNA)

WANT TO ESTABLISH A SENSE OF COMMUNITY HERE," SAID TERUYUKI *Minoura, president and CEO of Toyota Motor Manufacturing North America, Inc. (TMMNA), during a recent address at the company's new headquarters in Erlanger, Kentucky. "I sincerely look forward to building something special."* ▣ *TMMNA—whose employees are called team members—was established in 1996 as the U.S.-based* parent company of Toyota's rapidly expanding North American manufacturing operations, which had grown too large to be managed from Japan. Toyota has eight manufacturing facilities in North America, including a huge plant just down the road in Georgetown, Kentucky, which produces nearly 500,000 Camrys, Avalons, and Siennas each year. Toyota's manufacturing investment in the United States now totals approximately $11 billion. The ripple effect of this long-term economic commitment to North America has been felt in communities all across the country, including TMMNA's new Northern Kentucky home.

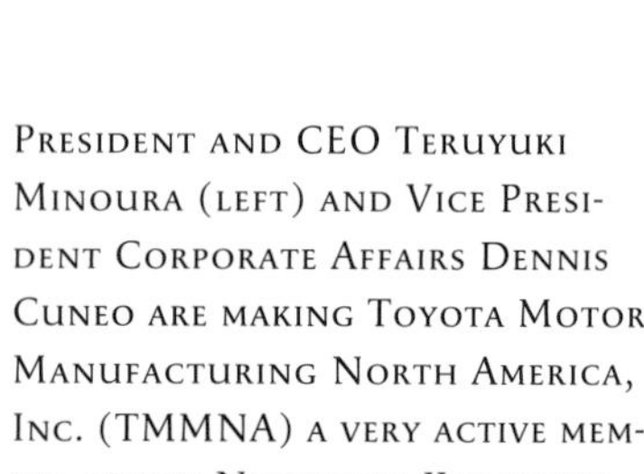

PRESIDENT AND CEO TERUYUKI MINOURA (LEFT) AND VICE PRESIDENT CORPORATE AFFAIRS DENNIS CUNEO ARE MAKING TOYOTA MOTOR MANUFACTURING NORTH AMERICA, INC. (TMMNA) A VERY ACTIVE MEMBER OF THE NORTHERN KENTUCKY COMMUNITY (TOP).

ONE OF TWO U.S. COMPANIES THAT PERFORM A HEADQUARTERS FUNCTION FOR TOYOTA, TMMNA CENTRALIZES KEY MANUFACTURING FUNCTIONS SUCH AS PURCHASING, PRODUCTION ENGINEERING, QUALITY CONTROL, AND PRODUCTION PLANNING UNDER ONE ROOF (BOTTOM).

Streamlining Operations

TMMNA is one of two U.S. companies that perform a headquarters function for Toyota. The other is Toyota Motor Sales (TMS) in Torrance, which manages the company's national network of 1,400 dealers and is responsible for sales and marketing of Toyota vehicles in North America. As the parent company for Toyota's North American manufacturing operations, TMMNA centralizes key manufacturing functions such as purchasing, production engineering, quality control, and production planning.

For example, Toyota's purchasing departments at each manufacturing plant used to buy their own parts, materials, services, and supplies directly, but now TMMNA has streamlined that process by consolidating North American purchasing at its headquarters office. Because the company annually buys more than $8 billion worth of goods and services from more than 500 North American suppliers, this consolidation brought with it significant economies of scale, helping to reduce costs.

Improved efficiency is another major benefit resulting from the establishment of TMMNA. With billions of dollars in construction and expansion projects under way across North America, TMMNA's engineering staff keeps everything under control.

The same is true for the production and quality control functions. Centralizing the production control process speeds decision making in production planning, and facilitates better coordination among the manufacturing plants and between the plants and suppliers. Similarly, quality control is enhanced because TMMNA assures common standards and consistent policies for plants and suppliers.

Economic Impact

There are many chapters in the story of Toyota's increasing manufacturing presence in North America, and the key element is jobs. TMMNA's drive to expand its production capacity in North

America to more than a million vehicles a year has generated thousands of jobs. A recent economic impact study from the University of Michigan concluded that every new job created by Toyota generates an additional 5.5 jobs downstream for other Americans. So, roughly speaking, Toyota's 20,000 manufacturing jobs in North America are actually responsible for more than 110,000 jobs overall.

Many of these downstream jobs are at Toyota's 500 U.S. parts and materials suppliers, such as Sachs Automotive in Florence, Kentucky, which supplies shocks and struts to Toyota's North American plants. But the impact is even more profound than that. Cincinnati Milacron, for example, has hired additional workers over the years to help fill orders from Toyota for dozens of huge, multimillion-dollar plastic injection molding machines. And Toyota contracts with several firms that provide various services, especially construction, a practice that results in jobs for thousands of Americans at Toyota's various North American construction projects.

Part of the Community

Toyota wants to build more and more of its vehicles in North America. Approximately 65 percent of Toyotas sold in North America are now built in North America, and that percentage is growing. As the fourth-largest U.S. automaker, Toyota believes its growth and continued success in the marketplace depend on its ability to understand and respect the unique qualities and different needs of people and their local communities. Giving this important task the time and attention it deserves is another important reason for the establishment of TMMNA.

"Toyota is determined to become an active member of our new Northern Kentucky community," said TMMNA Vice President Dennis Cuneo. "We've tried to demonstrate our good corporate citizenship through the volunteer activities of our team members as well as through company contributions to several worthwhile local projects."

Team members at TMMNA say they have found much to like about their new home. From its proximity to Toyota's U.S. supply base and manufacturing plants (which are concentrated in the Midwest and upper South), to its easy access to an international airport that provides direct connections to most places team members need to reach, this area has all the options Toyota wanted. Also attractive are the quality of life and welcome reception from new neighbors, which, Toyota has learned, are standard equipment in Northern Kentucky.

Since its establishment in 1996, TMMNA has helped to increase efficiency in automobile manufacturing. At its Georgetown, Kentucky, plant, robotic arms weld vehicle frames as they move down the assembly line (top left).

A team member positions a door on a Sienna minivan at Toyota's manufacturing facility in Georgetown, which produces nearly 500,000 vehicles each year (top right).

TMMNA's commitment to its community benefits even the smallest Northern Kentuckians.

Northern Kentucky Convention Center

LOCATED ON A STRETCH OF THE OHIO RIVER'S SOUTHERN SHORE, *where scores of exciting new developments are helping revitalize the historic city of Covington, the Northern Kentucky Convention Center has quickly established itself as a cornerstone for the region's exciting future.* ▣ *The gleaming, $30.5 million masonry and glass structure opened in November 1998 amid a buzz of construction* activity—a new, 15-story Marriott hotel across the street; a new, high-rise office tower; new county and federal courthouses a few blocks away; and Newport's aquarium and entertainment district just across the nearby Licking River. Similar progress is taking place across Northern Kentucky from the ground up—at all levels and in all directions. In fact, the convention center's opening has prompted many other important projects to fall into place.

THE NORTHERN KENTUCKY CONVENTION CENTER'S PRIMARY MISSION IS TO BE A CATALYST FOR REGIONAL ECONOMIC GROWTH. TO THAT END, THE FACILITY IS FOCUSED ON DRAWING ALL TYPES OF EVENTS TO THE AREA AND SHOWCASING A NEW NORTHERN KENTUCKY TO VISITORS, TOURISTS, AND NEIGHBORS.

A Catalyst for Economic Growth

It is no coincidence that the Northern Kentucky Convention Center was the first of the area's major new riverfront projects to open. It happened that way for good reason. The convention center's primary mission is to be a catalyst for regional economic growth. To that end, the facility is focused on drawing all types of events to the area and showcasing a new Northern Kentucky to visitors, tourists, and neighbors.

Besides economic stimulation, the convention center will serve the needs of Northern Kentucky's growing corporate community, much of which is headquartered in the twin RiverCenter office towers nearby. It will also complement the area's flourishing hotel and tourism industries.

Flexibility, Accessibility, and Service

The Northern Kentucky Convention Center offers 110,000 square feet of usable space for trade shows, exhibits, concerts, meetings, and banquets—including a 46,000-square-foot, first-floor exhibit hall (divisible into two smaller rooms) with 30-foot ceilings, as well as a 22,000-square-foot ballroom, 10 state-of-the-art meeting rooms, and a modern, fully equipped kitchen with full-service catering. The high-tech facility was built to adapt to emerging technologies, and offers satellite uplink/downlink, modem lines, and an in-house audiovisual company equipped to handle virtually any customer need. Adjacent to the convention center are more than 2,000 parking spaces.

Visitors can enter through a dramatic, three-story atrium that provides a sweeping view of the Ohio River and the impressive Cincinnati skyline. Adjacent lobbies provide nearly 20,000 square feet of carpeted public areas for registration or preliminary activities.

Accessibility is another key draw for the convention center. Situated right in the middle of Covington's bustling riverfront district, the facility is only a short trip across the historic Roebling Suspension Bridge from downtown Cincinnati. Additionally, it is only 10 minutes from the Cincinnati/Northern Kentucky International Airport and within walking distance of more than 500 hotel rooms, dozens of restaurants and nightclubs, Cinergy Field, and the new Paul Brown Stadium.

Another aspect of the convention center that visitors cannot help but notice is the unique level of service provided by the facility's friendly staff. In fact, the entire team believes it is their job to make every single visitor feel personally welcome.

Designed to handle as many as 750 events per year, the Northern Kentucky Convention Center is already proving to be an invaluable asset for Covington and all of Northern Kentucky as the area continues to expand in the new millennium.

THE CONVENTION CENTER HOUSES A 46,000-SQUARE-FOOT, FIRST-FLOOR EXHIBIT HALL (DIVISIBLE INTO TWO SMALLER ROOMS) WITH 30-FOOT CEILINGS, AS WELL AS A 22,000-SQUARE-FOOT BALLROOM, AND 10 STATE-OF-THE-ART MEETING ROOMS (BOTTOM LEFT AND RIGHT).

RECENT ADDITION TO THE HEART OF THE NORTHERN KENTUCKY community, GE Capital Information Technology Solutions (GECITS) is a global, one-source provider of integrated information technology (IT) infrastructure solutions that keeps businesses focused sharply on their objectives and challenges. With customers ranging from medium-sized enterprises to Fortune 500 multinational cor- porations, GECITS offers a full range of integrated technologies and services. These total integrated services help corporations overcome information technology challenges while meeting their business goals.

GECITS was formed in 1996, through the acquisition of Hamilton Computer Sales and Rentals in Canada, Ameridata in the United States, CompuNet in Germany, and Ferntree in Australia. In 1996, a consolidation of these operations led to the creation of GECITS as a global organization. A year after this consolidation, GECITS acquired an additional 14 companies.

Today, with recent acquisitions of XL Source in the United States, Ista in France, and P&P in the United Kingdom, GECITS has more than 150 locations in the United States, Canada, Mexico, and Brazil, as well as in 10 countries in Europe, including France, Germany, and the United Kingdom. The company maintains a presence on the Internet at www.gecits.ge.com.

This phase of consolidation and acquisition has also marked a shift in the business of GECITS, from hardware reseller to global integrated IT infrastructure solutions provider. The company is now one of the largest independent global suppliers of comprehensive information technology solutions. GECITS serves the oil and gas, financial, insurance, real estate, mining, manufacturing, communications, government, fishing, agriculture, transportation, wholesale, and retail markets with offerings in three strategic categories: business solutions, support solutions, and acquisition solutions.

GECITS focuses on producing better solutions for its customers, on employing talented people and constantly developing their skills, and on achieving Six Sigma quality in all of its millions of daily transactions. The firm has been able to reach high levels of excellence through its corporate structure, which allows departments to interact through a process of actions and impacts that are always tangible and measurable.

GECITS customers include brewing giant Labatt USA; consumer packaged goods leader Pezrow Companies Inc.; forestry company Weyerhaeuser; Eli Lilly Pharmaceuticals; and Mackenzie Financial Corp. For these and other companies, GECITS provides a range of services. For example, Labatt USA, a company that was growing very quickly, needed to have its computer network and infrastructure upgraded. GECITS implemented Microsoft products (NT Workstation and BackOffice) quickly and with minimal disruption to Labatt's day-to-day operations. With the new system, Labatt USA reduced its support costs, improved its network speed and performance, and enhanced communications between its employees and business partners.

Headquartered in Newport, Kentucky, GECITS offers a variety of solutions to support information technology needs in the areas of IT management services, E-commerce, internetworking architecture services, software licensing, asset management, enterprise management services, and disaster recovery. With offices in 15 countries around the world. GECITS is a GE Capital company, a diversified global financial services company with 28 specialized businesses. As part of the GE family of companies, GECITS is a valued member of an organization *Fortune* magazine voted as the Most Admired Company in America for the second consecutive year in 1999.

JAMES E. MOHN IS PRESIDENT AND CEO OF GE CAPITAL INFORMATION TECHNOLOGY SOLUTIONS (GECITS), A GLOBAL, ONE-SOURCE PROVIDER OF INTEGRATED IT INFRASTRUCTURE SOLUTIONS THAT KEEPS BUSINESSES FOCUSED SHARPLY ON THEIR OBJECTIVES AND CHALLENGES.

ILD FLAVORS IS A PRIVATELY HELD, RESPONSIVE, AND *entrepreneurially focused, full-service flavor and ingredient provider to the food and beverage industries. Originally, the company developed naturally derived fruit flavors for beverage manufacturers, but during the 1990s, with U.S. expansion, that focus changed. Today, WILD Flavors produces a full line of flavors and natural* colors for beverages, culinary products, sweet and baked goods, and pharmaceuticals.

To enhance its core activities in the flavor industry, the company also performs applications development with nutraceuticals, which are designed to add flavor and health-giving nutrients to foods and beverages. This aspect of the company has also evolved over the years: In a short time, WILD Flavors has developed a nutraceutical database and has mastered data retrieval and regulatory requirements and methods to add the components while maintaining the desired flavor and texture.

WILD Beginnings

WILD Flavors is a division of the WILD Group, founded and based in Heidelberg by Dr. Rudolf Wild in 1931. Today, the WILD Group is a strong international resource in the flavor industry, with offices and facilities in more than 50 countries and with more than 1,700 people around the globe.

The WILD Group recently expanded into North America, setting up facilities in the United States, Canada, and Mexico. The Erlanger, Kentucky, office is the firm's North American headquarters, and it oversees the manufacturing facilities, applications research, and sales and customer service teams in Canada, as well as the sales office and applications laboratory in Mexico.

WILD Flavors services a wide range of clients, from small, start-up companies with an entrepreneurial background to large, corporate multinationals with large market shares. "The company works very closely with its clients to develop products and product lines," says President and CEO Michael H. Ponder.

Though the company has broadened its focus, it has not changed its original corporation philosophy. Says Ponder, "We are very customer focused, and we take a full systems approach to providing accurate, innovative solutions for our customers."

SoBe: A Prominent Customer

One of WILD Flavors' most popular and widely recognized clients is South Beach Beverage Company, which produces the SoBe line of New Age, nutritionally enhanced beverages.

The SoBe beverage line debuted in 1996, marked by the trademark

WITH ITS NORTH AMERICAN HEADQUARTERS IN NORTHERN KENTUCKY, WILD FLAVORS IS A PRIVATELY HELD, RESPONSIVE, ENTREPRENEURIALLY FOCUSED, FULL-SERVICE FLAVOR AND INGREDIENT PROVIDER TO THE FOOD AND BEVERAGE INDUSTRIES.

WILD's knowledgeable and dedicated employees are committed to creating and providing innovative solutions to satisfy the customers' needs.

yin-yang lizards on the bottle. At that time, South Beach Beverage Company was a small, entrepreneurial endeavor by John Bello and Tom Schwalm. From the outset, South Beach sought out WILD Flavors to conduct an effort to differentiate the SoBe line from other similar drinks. WILD Flavors developed new and healthy drink flavors for SoBe, as well as packaging marketing, and product positioning. The effects of the collaboration were immediate: SoBe quickly became a front-runner in the alternative beverage industry.

Today, South Beach Beverage Company is one of the fastest-growing beverage companies in the United States, and SoBe is a highly successful product line, with a multitude of flavors, including—among many others—3C Elixirs, such as Orange-Carrot and Cranberry-Grapefruit; Black, Red, Green, and Oolong Teas; Zen Blend Tea with ginseng and schizandra; Wisdom with ginkgo, Saint John's Wort, and gotu kola; and Eros with dong quai, damiana, foti, and zinc. Working together, the two companies have produced one of the healthiest and most popular alternative drink lines in the United States.

A Commitment to Northern Kentucky

The WILD Flavors North American headquarters in Erlanger clearly represents the company's strong commitment to the Northern Kentucky community and to the flavor industry. Constructed in early 1998, the facility is a result of the company's goal to establish a strong presence in the United States while expanding globally.

Located near the Cincinnati/Northern Kentucky airport, the facility works as a selling point for the company. "As a company that's only been around for a couple of years, our initial challenge was getting people to know who we are and what we do," explains Ponder. "Bringing them here and showing them the facility, the high quality, and the advanced technology has been a strong sales tool, and it has helped us obtain a number of projects."

WILD Flavors places the highest value on the knowledge, capabilities, experience, and enthusiasm of the people within the company and the hospitality of the people who have welcomed the company to Northern Kentucky. The company currently employs more than 185.

Northern Kentucky also provides the company many opportunities to grow and expand, and WILD Flavors is a valuable corporate asset to the community.

Ashland Inc.

SINCE RELOCATING ITS HEADQUARTERS TO COVINGTON IN *January 1999, Ashland Inc. may be the new kid on the block in Northern Kentucky corporate circles, but its roots in the state run long and deep. Moreover, many of its diversified businesses have been well established in the Northern Kentucky/Greater Cincinnati market for decades.* *Founded by Paul G. Blazer in 1924 as an* oil-refining subsidiary of Lexington-based Swiss Oil Corporation, Ashland Inc. today is a multi-industry company with related businesses operating worldwide. Among them are four wholly owned divisions involved in chemical and plastics distribution, specialty chemicals, branded motor oil and car care products, and highway construction. Ashland Inc. also owns major stakes in a petroleum refining and marketing joint venture and in a coal production company.

Strategically Located in Covington

Considering Ashland's operations (including a large corporate office that remains in Ashland), one of the major reasons it chose to relocate its headquarters in Northern Kentucky is readily apparent. Geographically, Northern Kentucky is the hub of Ashland's operational wheel; the new office is encircled by its constituent parts.

Northeast from Ashland's Covington headquarters is Ashland Distribution Company, which is in Dublin, Ohio, near Columbus. This offshoot is the largest distributor of industrial chemicals and plastics in North America, and it operates more than 100 distribution centers in North America and Europe. Its annual sales exceed $3 billion.

Ashland Specialty Chemical Company is also based in Dublin. Reporting annual sales of more than $1.2 billion, it is a leading producer of six global lines of specialty chemicals, including foundry chemicals, adhesives, electronic chemicals, marine and water treatment chemicals, and polyester resins.

To the south of Ashland's Covington headquarters is The Valvoline Company, located in Lexington. Valvoline is a leading innovator and supplier of automotive products. Best known for Valvoline® motor oil, it also produces Zerex® antifreeze/coolant, SynPower® and Pyroil® automotive chemicals, and Eagle One® appearance products. The division operates more than 550 Valvoline Instant Oil Change service centers in 34 states, including 20 locally, as well as a motor oil packaging plant in Cincinnati. Valvoline's annual sales exceed $1 billion.

Ashland Inc. and Marathon Oil Company formed Marathon Ashland Petroleum LLC in 1998 by combining their major refining, marketing, and transportation operations. The result is one of the nation's largest refiners and an operator of 5,400 SuperAmerica, Speedway, Marathon, and Ashland gasoline/convenience stores in 20 states, including more than 100 outlets in the immediate area. It also operates a terminal on the Ohio River in Cincinnati, which was acquired as part of Ashland Inc.'s purchase of Tresler Oil several years ago. Based in Findlay, Ohio, the joint venture is 38 percent owned by Ashland. Speedway SuperAmerica's headquarters is just 70 miles away in Springfield, Ohio.

Based in nearby St. Louis, Arch Coal, Inc. was formed by the merger of Ashland Coal, Inc. and Arch Mineral Corporation in 1997, with Ashland Inc. maintaining a 58 percent equity interest. It is the

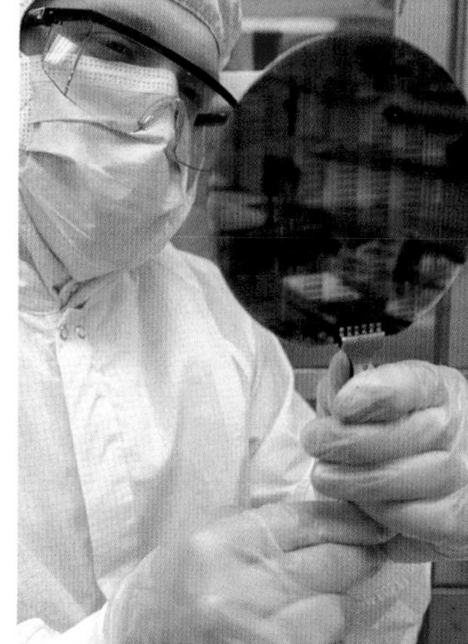

CLOCKWISE FROM TOP LEFT:
ON JANUARY 4, 1999, ASHLAND INC. RELOCATED ITS CORPORATE HEADQUARTERS TO THE TOWERS OF RIVERCENTER IN COVINGTON.

ULTRA-HIGH-PURITY CHEMICALS FOR THE SEMICONDUCTOR INDUSTRY IS JUST ONE OF THE MANY SPECIALTY CHEMICAL PRODUCTS OFFERED BY ASHLAND SPECIALTY CHEMICAL COMPANY.

COMPLEMENTING ARCH COAL'S VALUABLE LOW-SULFUR COAL RESERVES ARE HIGHLY EFFICIENT MINING OPERATIONS. ARCH'S COAL PRODUCTION FUELS ROUGHLY 6 PERCENT OF THE NATION'S ELECTRICITY NEEDS.

nation's second-largest producer of coal and the largest in the eastern United States. More than 85 percent of its sizable coal reserves are low-sulfur, and 60 percent meet the stringent federal clean-air standards effective in January 2000. The company has been a traditional supplier to local power companies.

Ashland's APAC construction group is the nation's largest highway paver and contractor. It builds interstate highways, bridges, residential streets, and commercial driveways in more than a dozen states in the South and Midwest. APAC is based in Atlanta and generates about $1.5 billion in annual sales.

Positioned for Performance

Ashland's mission is to be a high-performance, growth-oriented, world-class competitor operating a mix of related businesses that generate superior long-term returns for Ashland's shareholders. This goal was the impetus behind its decision to move its headquarters from Ashland, where it had flourished for nearly 75 years, 150 miles down river to Covington. Overlooking the booming Northern Kentucky riverfront, the company's new home is not more than a two-hour drive or a nonstop flight from any of Ashland's businesses. The company plans to maintain its historic and valued ties to Kentucky. Besides its operations

in Ashland and Lexington, Ashland Inc. still maintains gasoline and asphalt storage terminals in Louisville.

Ashland's notable strengths include leading market-share positions in most of its businesses; efficient, low-cost production capabilities; marketing and distribution networks with critical mass and economies of scale; superior product quality and customer focus; and a long tradition of product innovation.

"In business units where these advantages don't exist, we will create them or consider applying our resources elsewhere," says Paul W. Chellgren, Ashland's chairman and chief executive officer.

Chellgren notes with pride that Ashland has in recent years recast itself as a streamlined company with critical mass in a number of related industries. It inaugurates the 21st century geared for a new era of performance and driven by a desire to deliver value for shareholders; quality products and services for its customers; a challenging work environment for its employees; and positive, responsible, and ethical actions for the communities in which it operates.

Ashland's headquarters staff in Covington numbers only about 100 people, but the "new kids" plan to make an important impact on Northern Kentucky and their adopted communities. The company was attracted to this area by a wealth of local assets—including the arts, sports, and entertainment communities, as well as the quality schools and the area's natural beauty—and its employees are eagerly planning to contribute to the continued prosperity of their new communities. It will surely be with the same drive and gusto that they apply to Ashland's corporate affairs.

Clockwise from top left: About 2 million credit card customers enjoy the brands offered by Marathon Ashland Petroleum, including Marathon, Ashland, Speedway, and SuperAmerica.

From race car drivers to teens with their first cars, people who know use Valvoline.

Ashland's APAC construction group enjoys market leadership in both asphalt and concrete paving, and is a major player in aggregate production and the construction materials market.

Towery Publishing, Inc.

EGINNING AS A SMALL PUBLISHER OF LOCAL NEWSPAPERS IN THE *1930s, Towery Publishing, Inc. today produces a wide range of community-oriented materials, including books (Urban Tapestry Series), business directories, magazines, and Internet publications. Building on its long heritage of excellence, the company has become global in scope, with cities from San Diego to Sydney* represented by Towery products. In all its endeavors, this Memphis-based company strives to be synonymous with service, utility, and quality.

A Diversity of Community-Based Products

Over the years, Towery has become the largest producer of published materials for North American chambers of commerce. From membership directories that enhance business-to-business communication to visitor and relocation guides tailored to reflect the unique qualities of the communities they cover, the company's chamber-oriented materials offer comprehensive information on dozens of topics, including housing, education, leisure activities, health care, and local government.

In 1998, the company acquired Cincinnati-based Target Marketing, an established provider of detailed city street maps to more than 300 chambers of commerce throughout the United States and Canada. Now a division of Towery, Target offers full-color maps that include local landmarks and points of interest, such as parks, shopping centers, golf courses, schools, industrial parks, city and county limits, subdivision names, public buildings, and even block numbers on most streets.

In 1990, Towery launched the Urban Tapestry Series, an award-winning collection of oversized, hardbound photojournals detailing the people, history, culture, environment, and commerce of various metropolitan areas. These coffee-table books highlight a community through three basic elements: an introductory essay by a noted local individual; an exquisite collection of four-color photographs; and profiles of the companies and organizations that animate the area's business life.

To date, more than 80 Urban Tapestry Series editions have been published in cities around the world, from New York to Vancouver to Sydney. Authors of the books' introductory essays include former U.S. President Gerald Ford (Grand Rapids), former Alberta Premier Peter Lougheed (Calgary), CBS anchor Dan Rather (Austin), ABC anchor Hugh Downs (Phoenix), best-selling mystery author Robert B. Parker (Boston), American Movie Classics host Nick Clooney (Cincinnati), Senator Richard Lugar (Indianapolis), and Challenger Center founder June Scobee Rodgers (Chattanooga).

To maintain hands-on quality in all of its periodicals and books, Towery has long used the latest production methods available. The company was the first production environment in the United States to combine desktop publishing with color separations and image scanning to produce finished film suitable for burning plates for four-color printing. Today, Towery relies on state-of-the-art digital prepress services to produce more than 8,000 pages each year, containing well over 30,000 high-quality color images.

◀ STEVE DAVIS

Towery Publishing President and CEO J. Robert Towery has expanded the business his parents started in the 1930s to include a growing array of traditional and electronic published materials, as well as Internet and multimedia services, that are marketed locally, nationally, and internationally.

An Internet Pioneer

By combining its long-standing expertise in community-oriented published materials with advanced production capabilities, a global sales force, and extensive data management expertise, Towery has emerged as a significant provider of Internet-based city information. In keeping with its overall focus on community resources, the company's Internet efforts represent a natural step in the evolution of the business.

The primary product lines within the Internet division are the introCity™ sites. Towery's introCity sites introduce newcomers, visitors,

▲ JONATHAN POSTAL

and long-time residents to every facet of a particular community, while simultaneously placing the local chamber of commerce at the forefront of the city's Internet activity. The sites include newcomer information, calendars, photos, citywide business listings with everything from nightlife to shopping to family fun, and online maps pinpointing the exact location of businesses, schools, attractions, and much more.

Decades of Publishing Expertise

In 1972, current President and CEO J. Robert Towery succeeded his parents in managing the printing and publishing business they had founded nearly four decades earlier. Soon thereafter, he expanded the scope of the company's published materials to include Memphis magazine and other successful regional and national publications. In 1985, after selling its locally focused assets, Towery began the trajectory on which it continues today, creating community-oriented materials that are often produced in conjunction with chambers of commerce and other business organizations.

Despite the decades of change, Towery himself follows a longstanding family philosophy of unmatched service and unflinching quality. That approach extends throughout the entire organization to include more than 130 employees at the Memphis headquarters, another 60 located in Northern Kentucky outside Cincinnati, and more than 50 sales, marketing, and editorial staff travelling to and working in a growing list of client cities. All of its products, and more information about the company, are featured on the Internet at www.towery.com.

In summing up his company's steady growth, Towery restates the essential formula that has driven the business since its first pages were published: "The creative energies of our staff drive us toward innovation and invention. Our people make the highest possible demands on themselves, so I know that our future is secure if the ingredients for success remain a focus on service and quality."

Towery Publishing was the first production environment in the United States to combine desktop publishing with color separations and image scanning to produce finished film suitable for burning plates for four-color printing. Today, the company's state-of-the-art network of Macintosh and Windows workstations allows it to produce more than 8,000 pages each year, containing more than 30,000 high-quality color images (top).

The Towery family's publishing roots can be traced to 1935, when R.W. Towery (far left) began producing a series of community histories in Tennessee, Mississippi, and Texas. Throughout the company's history, the founding family has consistently exhibited a commitment to clarity, precision, innovation, and vision (bottom).

Library of Congress Cataloging-in-Publication Data

Cauthen, Steve, 1960-
Northern Kentucky : looking to the new millennium / by Steve Cauthen ; art direction by Enrique Espinosa ; sponsored by the Northern Kentucky Chamber of Commerce.
p. cm. — (Urban tapestry series)
Includes index.
ISBN 1-881096-74-2 (alk. paper)
1. Kentucky—Civilization. 2. Kentucky—Pictorial works. 3. Kentucky—Economic conditions. 4. Business enterprises—Kentucky. 5. Cincinnati Region (Ohio)—Civilization. 6. Cincinnati Region (Ohio)—Pictorial works. 7. Cincinnati Region (Ohio)—Economic conditions. 8. Business enterprises—Ohio—Cincinnati Region. I. Title. II. Series.
F456.2.C38 1999
976.9—dc21

99-049625

Publisher: J. Robert Towery ▪ Executive Publisher: Jenny McDowell ▪ National Sales Manager: Stephen Hung ▪ Marketing Director: Carol Culpepper ▪ Project Directors: Mary Hanley, Carolyn Troescher ▪ Executive Editor: David B. Dawson ▪ Managing Editor: Lynn Conlee ▪ Senior Editor: Carlisle Hacker ▪ Editor/Profile Manager: Stephen Deusner ▪ Editors: Mary Jane Adams, Jana Files, Brian Johnston, Ginny Reeves, Sunni Thompson ▪ Assistant Editor: Rebecca Green ▪ Profile Writer: Jack Neff ▪ Editorial Contributor: Daryl Knauer ▪ Caption Writer: Grete Samsa ▪ Creative Director: Brian Groppe ▪ Photography Editor: Jonathan Postal ▪ Photographic Consultant: Mark Bowen ▪ Photography Coordinator: Robin Lankford ▪ Profile Designers: Laurie Beck, Melissa Ellis, Kelley Pratt, Ann Ward ▪ Production Assistants: Loretta Drew ▪ Production Resources Manager: Dave Dunlap Jr. ▪ Production Manager: Brenda Pattat ▪ Digital Color Supervisor: Darin Ipema ▪ Digital Color Technicians: Amanda Bozeman, Eric Friedl, Deidre Kesler, Brent Salazar ▪ Print Coordinator: Tonda Thomas ▪

Towery Publishing, Inc.
The Towery Building, 1835 Union Avenue
Memphis, TN 38104

PHOTOGRAPHERS

Allsport was founded the moment freelance photographer Tony Duffy captured the now-famous picture of Bob Beamon breaking the world long-jump record at the Mexico City Olympics in 1968. Originally headquartered in London, Allsport has expanded to include offices in New York and Los Angeles. Its pictures have appeared in every major publication in the world, and the best of its portfolio has been displayed at elite photographic exhibitions at the Royal Photographic Society and the Olympic Museum in Lausanne.

Roger Bickel is a Bingham Farms, Michigan, freelance photographer who specializes in travel and nature stock photography. His photos include images from most of the 50 states and the flora and fauna of Michigan. Bickel's work has appeared in a number of Towery publications, including *Cincinnati: Crowning Glory; Dayton: The Cradle of Creativity; Discover Columbus;* and *Greater Detroit: Renewing the Dream.* His photographs have also appeared in *National Geographic Explorer, Better Homes and Gardens, Woman's World,* Delta Airlines' *Sky*, and books by Houghton Mifflin, Barnes and Noble, Insight Guides, and Children's Press.

Chris Cone received his bachelor of arts degree from Denison University. He specializes in photographing people on location, and his photographs have been used by corporations, trade publications, health care professionals, ad agencies, and design firms.

L.J. Franklin, originally from Oklahoma City, moved to Cincinnati in 1985, where she is a teacher for Wyoming City Schools. Franklin has had one-woman shows at the Cincinnati Nature Center, the Mt. Adams Bookstore, Kaldi's Coffee House and Bookstore, and the Olmes Gallery. She enjoys photographing close-ups in nature, experimenting with Polaroid transfers and Polaroid SX-70, and travel photography.

© BUD LEE

Jane Gahl received a bachelor of arts degree in industrial design from the University of Cincinnati. Retired, she focuses on photography as a hobby. Gahl's images have been included in the *Maple Knoll Village 150th Anniversary Annual Report* and *International Photographer Magazine.*

Jim Hurtle is a data communications analyst with Procter & Gamble. He is a member of the Tri-State Photographic Society, and received a degree in electrical engineering from Oklahoma State University.

Dorothy Johnston is a freelance writer and photographer for the *Cincinnati Post* and the *Kentucky Post.* She won the 1996 Kentucky Press Association award for best feature story in a class III weekly. Johnston specializes in event photography and feature story journalism.

Gail Kissinger attended Miami University and the Kazik Pazovsky School of Photography. Her images have appeared in *Community Press* newspapers, *Ohio Lawyers Weekly*, and *Home Health Care Magazine.* Kissinger owns and operates Cincinnati-based Gail Kissinger Photography, and specializes in location and environmental portraiture.

Bud Lee studied at the Columbia University School of Fine Arts in New York and the National Academy of Fine Arts before moving to the Orlando area more than 20 years ago. A self-employed photojournalist, he founded both the Florida Photographers Workshop and the Iowa Photographers Workshop. Lee's work can be seen in *Esquire, Life, Travel & Leisure, Rolling Stone,* the *Washington Post,* and the *New York Times,* as well as in Towery Publishing's *Treasures on Tampa Bay: Tampa, St. Petersburg, Clearwater; Orlando: The City Beautiful; Jacksonville: Reflections of Excellence; Greater Syracuse: Center of an Empire; Los Angeles: City of Dreams;* and *St. Louis: For the Record.*

Mary Nemeth is a teacher with the Forest Hills School District, as well as owner of Nemeth Photography. Her images have appeared in *Popular Photo, Outdoor Photography,* and *Peterson's Photographic.* Nemeth is originally from South Bend.

Norton Photostock is a division of Norton Photography 2, an established, premier commercial, editorial, and advertising studio serving the Greater Cincinnati and Northern Kentucky market since 1989. The agency maintains an extensive file of more than 20,000 images of people, places, and events.

Photophile, established in San Diego in 1967, is owned and operated by Nancy Likins-Masten. An internationally known stock photography agency, the company houses more than 1 million color images, and represents more than 90 contributing local and international photographers. Subjects include extensive coverage of the West Coast, business/industry, people/lifestyles, health/medicine, travel, scenics, wildlife, and adventure sports, plus 200 additional categories.

Anne Pinnau, a graduate of Ohio University, has been a photographer for the *Middletown Journal*, an advertising photographer for Makro, Inc., and the public relations photographer for the Jewish Hospital. She is currently the corporate photographer for the Health Alliance of Greater Cincinnati. Pinnau has done freelance work for local businesses, as well as for various national magazines.

Carl Schmitt, originally from Detroit, has lived in various small towns in western, central, and southeastern Michigan. He moved to Northern Kentucky about 11 years ago. Schmitt has won numerous awards in competitions held by local clubs. Presently, his work is part of *Kentucky Moment VII*, on display at the Kentucky State Capitol.

Dan Tye is a freelance professional photographer with 17 years of experience. He is a native of Cincinnati, and many of his photographs focus on regional points of interest in the Midwest. Tye has traveled across the United States to photograph wildlife in their natural habitat. He specializes in landscapes and nature scenes.

Tom Uhlman, a native of Cincinnati, specializes in sports and outdoor photography. He enjoys spelunking and kayaking in his spare time.

Dale Voelker has won photography awards in numerous competitions, including those held by Cumberland Falls and Pine Mountain State Park. He photographed 47 events during the Kentucky bicentennial celebration in 1992. Voelker attended the University of Cincinnati.

Bruce Wess owns and operates the Burlington, Kentucky-based Wild Walks Photography. He worked as a school psychologist for 17 years prior to starting his photography business. Wess has received degrees from Princeton University and the University of Minnesota.

William West is an amateur photographer, contributing his time and energy to the Hamilton County Park District and the Southwestern Ohio Historical Society. His favorite subjects are nature, insects, and amphibians.

Keith Youtcheff received an associate's degree from Antonelli College of Art and Photography. He recently won six ribbons at the Kentucky Professional Photographers Convention, bringing his grand total to 21. Youtcheff enjoys photographing wildlife, and spent February 1999 capturing the beauty of Antarctica.

Additional organizations that contributed to *Northern Kentucky: Looking to the New Millennium* include Behringer-Crawford Museum, the Cincinnati Museum Center, and GeoIMAGERY.

▶ © BUD LEE

▶ © BUD LEE

WE MAY DOZE
BUT
NEVER CLOSE
HELP
WANTED

INDEX OF PROFILES

© BUD LEE